NEW ESTIMATES OF FERTILITY AND POPULATION IN THE UNITED STATES

NEW ESTIMATES
OF FERTILITY
AND POPULATION
IN THE UNITED STATES

A Study of Annual White Births from 1855 to 1960
and of Completeness of Enumeration in
the Censuses from 1880 to 1960

BY

ANSLEY J. COALE AND MELVIN ZELNIK

PRINCETON, NEW JERSEY
PRINCETON UNIVERSITY PRESS
1963

Publication of this book has been aided
by the Whitney Darrow Publication Reserve Fund
of Princeton University Press.

Printed in the United States of America
by The Maple Press Company, York, Penna.

Preface

This book is the consequence of a suggestion that Coale made to Zelnik in 1956 when the latter was a graduate student in sociology at Princeton University. Each student was required to complete a research project—a second-year paper—and Coale suggested that Zelnik analyze single-year age heaping in the decennial censuses of the United States since 1880 in a manner analogous to Coale's work on 5-year age heaping in an article he had published in 1955.[1] Zelnik's analysis showed conclusively that there had been a very nearly linear trend in age heaping at almost every age, for males and females alike, in the censuses from 1880 to 1950.[2] The existence of these linear trends made it feasible to estimate single-year age distributions of the native white populations in each census from 1880 to 1950—age distributions nearly free of the effects of age heaping.

The success of this early research led to a second suggestion by Coale—that Zelnik project these single-year age distributions (for females) back to birth to form estimates of white births and birth rates for years prior to the completion of the Birth Registration Area. This expanded research project became Zelnik's doctoral dissertation, written under Coale's supervision. Upon the completion of Zelnik's thesis in 1958, it was apparent that two types of extension should be attempted—births should be estimated from enumerated males as well as females, and the final adjusted birth estimates should be used to determine the approximate completeness of enumeration of each native white age group in each decennial census. In 1958–59, Wang Nai Chi, who was then a research aide at the Office of Population Research, calculated preliminary birth estimates from the male age distributions. In 1960–61, Marion O'Connor, also a research aide, made preliminary estimates of completeness of enumera-

[1] Ansley J. Coale, "The Population of the United States in 1950 Classified by Age, Sex, and Color—A Revision of Census Figures," *Journal of the American Statistical Association*, Vol. L (March 1955), pp. 16–54.

[2] This analysis was described in Melvin Zelnik, "Age Heaping in the United States Census: 1880–1950," *Milbank Memorial Fund Quarterly*, Vol. XXXIX, No. 3 (July 1961), pp. 540–573, as well as in Chapter 7 below.

tion. During the academic year 1961–62 Zelnik returned to the Office of Population Research as a research associate to collaborate with Coale in completing the analysis and composing the manuscript of this book.

We wish to express our gratitude to Mr. Wang and Mrs. O'Connor for the high quality of their work, and to Erna Härm, who restored to unified order a large volume of unverified calculations which had been made by divers persons over a period of several years. Mrs. Härm (a research aide at the Office) has also contributed to our research and analysis during the past year. The figures were drawn by Maria Martin and Daphne Notestein. The various drafts of the manuscript were edited and proofread by Margaret MacDonald. We gratefully acknowledge the helpful comments and suggestions made by Simon Kuznets, P. K. Whelpton, and Irene Taeuber.

A subvention from the National Science Foundation (G-17680) defrayed many of the extra expenses entailed in completing this project during the past year. In addition, the general support the Office of Population Research enjoys from the Rockefeller Foundation and the Milbank Memorial Fund was essential to its completion. We wish also to thank the Fund for permission to use, in its present form, the material contained in Chapter 7. The final responsibility for errors and shortcomings in this book rests with the authors.

MELVIN ZELNIK
ANSLEY J. COALE

Contents

vii

Tables

Figures

xiii

Part I

INTRODUCTION AND OUTLINE OF METHODS

Chapter 1. Introduction

Anyone interested in the demographic history of the United States, or in using its demographic data, is faced with many gaps and shortcomings in the published population records. One of the most prominent gaps is the lack of an annual series of births and birth rates covering the nineteenth century and the early part of the twentieth. A conspicuous shortcoming is inaccuracy in the decennial censuses of population, including incomplete enumeration and inaccurate reporting of age. These two deficiencies in the data are, in fact, intimately related—an annual series of births for some years in the past plus appropriate estimates of mortality would make it possible to determine the numbers of people who should have been enumerated at various ages in the censuses, since the censuses record the native population by single years of age from 1880 to 1950. Conversely, complete and accurate census age distributions, again with the appropriate estimates of mortality, would make it possible to estimate the number of births in the years preceding the census, because the enumerated native population consists of the survivors of these births.

Birth statistics purporting to cover the total United States did not become available until 1933, when the Birth Registration Area first included all states. Before that date there are statistics for some states, a few having data extending back to the early and mid-1800's. "Generalizing" these data to apply to the total United States requires the solution of two major problems: (1) that of representativeness—the statistics of these states may not reflect the fertility experience of other states and areas—and (2) the problem of unknown and changing degrees of under-registration in those states where records of registered births are available. For reasons which need not be detailed here, it is extremely doubtful that the fertility behavior in the states for which early data are available was in fact representative of the fertility behavior of the total population of the United States; nor does there seem to be any way of estimating the magnitude or pattern of differences between the fertility in those areas for which data are available and the fertility in those areas for which such data are not available.

Under-registration in the nineteenth century has been stud-

1

ied for one state, Massachusetts, where the estimated under-registration ranged from 18 per cent in 1850 to 3.3 per cent in 1890.[1] Although there is no direct evidence, it is highly probable that the birth registration completeness was similarly variable in other states. Even if the data available for these states were representative of the entire population, the large and inconstant incompleteness of registration would make birth estimates based on such registration of little value.[2]

Errors in the reported numbers of persons at each age in the censuses are of two types, logically, but not necessarily empirically, identifiable and distinguishable. One type of error is under- (or over-) reporting of the entire population or of persons of a particular age; the other is age misreporting. Under-enumeration appears to occur at all ages and to change gradually from one age to the next. "Age heaping"—the most conspicuous form of age misreporting—occurs positively at some ages, negatively at others immediately adjacent, resulting in sharp peaks and dips in the age distribution. Births estimated from these saw-toothed age distributions would exhibit the same spurious sharp rises and falls.

The absence of birth statistics has prevented a close analysis of the interrelationships between demographic and various social, economic, and political factors. An annual series of births and birth rates would not only reveal the past course of fertility in the United States, but it would make possible the testing of certain previously untestable hypotheses. The inaccuracy of census enumerations has meant that conclusions based on census data, including per capita rates such as death rates, have been erroneous, and to an unknown degree. In some instances, the size of the error involved is small and of only minor significance;

[1] Robert Gutman, "The Birth Statistics of Massachusetts During the Nineteenth Century," *Population Studies*, Vol. X, No. 1 (July 1956), p. 76, Table 2.

[2] The annual series of total United States births extending back to 1909 prepared for the National Office of Vital Statistics by P. K. Whelpton is essentially an attempt at using the birth statistics for various states. Although Whelpton's methods are highly sophisticated and ingenious, there is reason to believe his estimates are, as Whelpton himself recognized, subject to an increasing degree of error for the earlier years in this interval; and he attempted no estimates for years prior to 1909. For a detailed discussion of Whelpton's methods, see U.S. National Office of Vital Statistics, "Births and Birth Rates in the Entire United States 1909–1948," prepared by P. K. Whelpton, *Vital Statistics—Special Reports*, Vol. 33, No. 8 (1950).

in other instances, the error may be much larger and may have led to seriously defective conclusions. Estimates of census errors would provide greater precision as well as increased confidence and peace of mind to the researcher using census data.

This book is an attempt to fill these gaps in United States demographic data by providing estimates of annual births and birth rates for the white population of the United States back to the 1850's, and by providing estimates of census enumeration errors, by age and sex, for the native white and total white populations enumerated in the decennial censuses from 1880 to 1950.[3] The general procedure followed is simple in outline: the native white populations enumerated in each of the censuses from 1880 to 1950[4] were first adjusted for age heaping by single years of age separately for each sex; these adjusted populations were then projected backwards, using appropriate estimates of mortality, to the time of birth. As a consequence of using males and females as enumerated in several censuses, several estimates of births are obtained for each year; the various estimates were then combined to produce one annual series of total white births.[5] The survivors of these births were then projected forward to every census in which they were subsequently enumerated, to provide the expected population at each age. The differences between the expected populations and the enumerated populations provided estimates of the errors in the census counts of the native whites.[6]

---

[3] It has not been possible to prepare estimates of the census enumeration errors for the native whites enumerated in the 1960 census as the necessary data from that census were not available at the time this work was being done. It has, however, been possible to provide preliminary estimates of the undercounts of total whites for the 1960 census. A future article will cover the 1960 census when the required age distributions become available.

[4] The year 1880 was picked as the starting point because of the poor quality of the 1870 census and because censuses prior to that date do not contain the necessary single-year age distributions.

[5] Fortunately, nativity in the United States does not depend on the origin of the parents. Also, except for the population residing overseas in recent years (largely for military service), emigration of native Americans appears to have been negligible. Thus international migration does not disturb our calculations to a consequential degree.

[6] This very general and oversimplified statement might lead the reader to suspect some circularity in the reasoning employed and to wonder how a calculation, in which a population is projected backward and then forward, could result in a figure differing from the original. The details are explained in the subsequent chapters; at this point we can only say that the question of circularity is apparent rather than real and that the figures do differ for legitimate reasons.

3

The foreign-born whites, who constituted a small proportion of the total whites in 1950 and larger proportions in the preceding censuses, were adjusted by attributing to each age-sex census group the same proportionate error that had been found for the comparable native white group.

The actual working out of the different sets of estimates has been much more complicated and involved than this bare outline suggests. In the following chapters the methods used are described twice: first in a simple, non-technical way and then in a detailed, technical manner. Readers less interested in the details and more interested in the results will be able to find what they want without having to dig through the technical discussions and manipulations which are likely to be of interest only to specialists. Chapter 2 presents a non-technical summary of our method; Chapter 3 presents single-year estimates of births and birth rates and analyzes deviations from the long-term trend; Chapter 4 describes the long-term trend in fertility in comparison with trends in selected European countries; and Chapter 5 is a non-technical summary of estimated undercounts in the decennial censuses. Chapter 6 discusses the relation between the birth rate and the total fertility rate. Much of this chapter is very technical and will be of interest only to professional demographers. The non-technical reader is advised to read Part I (Chapter 2) and Part II (Chapters 3, 4 and 5). Part III (Chapters 6, 7, 8 and 9) contains detailed descriptions of the techniques of estimation. Appendices A and B describe special procedures and adjustments, and Appendix C contains detailed tables.

Chapter 2. General Statement of Methods

The two major results we have obtained are estimates of annual white births in the United States from 1855 to 1934 (after which estimates based on registration are adequate) and estimated single-year age distributions, for each sex, of the native white population at the time of each census from 1880 to 1950. The estimated age distributions are incomplete, terminating at age 29 in 1880, 39 in 1890, 49 in 1900, 58 in 1910, and extending to age 98 in 1950.[1]

The estimates of births and the estimated single-year age distributions are products of essentially the same analytical procedure. The purpose of this chapter is to give a brief and non-technical description of how both sets of estimates were derived. Readers interested in a more detailed and precise description of techniques are referred to Chapters 6 through 9.

The basic data on which all of our estimates were based are the single-year age distributions of the native white population recorded in the censuses of 1880 to 1950. Each birth class (or *cohort*) born between 1855 and 1934 was enumerated in several censuses. For every such cohort, we have estimated the proportion that could be expected to survive each intercensal decade. Consequently, it is possible to estimate the number of births that should have occurred *a* years before a given census in order to account for the persons enumerated at age *a* in that census. Such estimates are possible because there are tabulations (beginning in 1880) of the native white American population in single-year age distributions, and because losses through emigration of native Americans appear to have been numerically negligible, except for persons (primarily in military service) residing abroad in 1920 and 1950.

If the single-year age distributions of the native population in the decennial censuses were accurate and if mortality records were adequate to support accurate estimates of proportions surviving each decade, it would be possible to determine the annual births with precision. Actually, it has proven necessary

---

[1] The oldest four single-year estimates in the first three censuses, and the oldest three single-year estimates in the remaining censuses, are based on estimates of births from 1851–1854, which appear to be defective, and must consequently be viewed with some skepticism.

to resort to many adjustments and approximations, which are discussed below.

Adjustments for Age Heaping

Even a superficial examination of census data reveals systematic tendencies on the part of the enumerated population to report certain preferred ages. When a preferred age is reported, a less popular age is necessarily omitted. Ages ending in zero, five, and, to a lesser degree, in even numbers have been reported most frequently, while odd numbers (other than five) have typically been avoided. This characteristic age heaping is a major source of inaccuracy in distributions by single-years of age. It is not a deficiency that can be overcome by "smoothing" the age distribution or by fitting it by some simple functional form, because curve-fitting or age-smoothing would level out real differences in the size of consecutive age-groups, as well as spurious differences caused by preference and avoidance of particular ages.

It was possible to construct our birth estimates only after devising a satisfactory technique by which the extent of age heaping could be estimated, and its effects removed. This technique depends on a trend that we observed as prevailing in the interval 1880–1950—an approximately linear change over this interval in the proportion falsely choosing (or avoiding) each age. For example, about 33 per cent of females reported at age 40 in 1890 actually had some other age, about 25 per cent in 1910, 17 per cent in 1930, and 9 per cent in 1950.

The basic measure from which these estimates were derived was the number of persons reported at a given age relative to the average number reported in the five neighboring ages on each side. To establish the linear trends in age heaping, it was necessary to make allowance for the fact that the ratios just described are also affected by genuinely large or small age-groups, arising, for example, from a particularly large birth cohort immediately after a war. In this chapter we shall simply assert, without giving further evidence, that the progression of age heaping for almost every age does indeed appear to have been linear during the interval 1880–1950. The evidence is shown in graphic form in Figures 37 to 46, and discussed in detail in Chapter 7.

It was by fitting a straight line to a measure of age heaping in the different censuses that we derived estimates of the amount of preference or avoidance for each age in each individual census. These estimates of preference and avoidance were then employed to calculate census age-distributions *adjusted for age heaping* (see Figures 49 to 56).

Estimates of Mortality

The adjusted census age distributions of the native white population provide approximate measures of the size of each birth cohort at decennial intervals. If the proportion surviving each decade can be estimated, it becomes possible to estimate the size of each cohort at birth, i.e., the number of white births occurring each year. For example, assume that the number of native white females enumerated at age 36 in 1950 is approximately correct when adjusted for age heaping; then through successive division by the proportion surviving from age 26 to 36 in the decade of the 1940's, the proportion surviving from 16 to 26 in the 1930's, from 6 to 16 in the 1920's, and from birth to age 6 during 1913 to 1920, we can estimate white female births in 1913 (i.e., 36 to 37 years prior to the 1950 census). The ratio of male to female births is virtually constant, so that white male births, and consequently total white births, for 1913 could be estimated from the native white female aged 36 in the 1950 census. 1913 births could also be estimated from the number of *males* enumerated at age 36 in 1950 and from enumerations (of each sex) at age 26 in the 1940 census, 16 in the 1930 census, and 6 in the 1920 census. From the four censuses and two sexes there would be eight estimates—from eight different enumerated groups—of white births in 1913.

To make these estimates requires the availability of mortality records, so that proportions surviving may be determined. From 1900 on there are mortality rates by age for the Death Registration Area, which included ten states (and the District of Columbia) with about 26 per cent of the U.S. population in 1900, and thirty-four states (plus the District of Columbia) with about 80 per cent by 1920. We based our estimates of survivorship on these data. In 1929–1931, there were mortality tables prepared for the continental United States, and for the states that fell within the Death Registration Area at various earlier dates.

7

Differences in proportions surviving were almost negligible. We have made slight adjustments to estimated proportions surviving in the United States by assuming that relations of mortality in early Death Registration Area states to mortality in the entire United States were the same as in 1929–1931.

There are few mortality records for the nineteenth century in the United States. It was nevertheless possible to construct plausible estimates of proportions surviving in each decade from 1850 to 1900 because of the following facts:

1. Among populations of Western Europe and of predominantly West European origin (i.e., the United States, Canada, Australia, and New Zealand) mortality rates in different age intervals are highly intercorrelated. As a consequence of the intercorrelations, it is possible to estimate closely the mortality rate in each age interval in one of these populations from an index of the general level of mortality—the expectation of life at birth.

2. The increase in the expectation of life at birth in the United States in the interval 1900–1950 very closely paralleled the average experience of six of the Western European countries having mortality records back to 1850. It is likely that the parallel experience extended back to the last half of the nineteenth century.

3. An estimate of the expectation of life at birth in the United States in 1850 for each sex has been made on the basis of mortality data for Massachusetts and Maryland.[2] These estimates agree almost precisely with the average in 1850 in these six West European countries (Figure 1).

In the light of these facts, the Jacobson estimate of the expectation of life in the United States in 1850 was accepted. (It would have made no difference had we used the average of the six West European countries that paralleled the United States experience after 1900.) A linear rise in expectation of life at birth from 1850 to 1900 was assumed. Finally, the typical West European relation between mortality at each age and expectation of life at birth was used to estimate proportions surviving in each age interval.

[2] Paul H. Jacobson, "An Estimate of the Expectation of Life in the United States in 1850," Milbank Memorial Fund *Quarterly*, Vol. XXXV, No. 2, (April 1957), pp. 197–201.

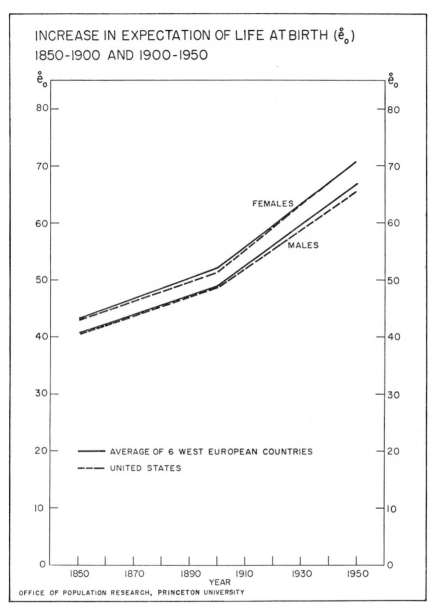

FIGURE 1.   Expectation of Life at Birth $(\mathring{e}_0)$, by Sex, in the United States and Average of Six West European Countries, 1850, 1900, 1950.

Mortality Adjustments for Wartime Losses

Records of war-connected deaths for men in military service appear sufficient for World War I and World War II to permit estimates of proportions of males surviving from 1910 to 1920 and 1940 to 1950, even for those male cohorts that were of military age during each war. Though these records may be somewhat inaccurate, the effect on our estimates is probably not serious, since the largest losses in any single age-group are only about 7 per cent; even if estimated war losses are 10 per cent in error, the effect on the estimated number of births would be only 0.7 per cent.

The Civil War is a different story. War deaths amounted to much larger fractions of men at the ages of military service, and no reliable records of the number of deaths exist. Consequently, we cannot project backwards any males at ages that would have been subject to military service in the Civil War. This restriction means that the earliest births that can be estimated from enumerated males are those of 1851. Although females were not subject to "excess mortality" caused by military service, birth estimates from females also could not be extended to the years prior to 1851, because of undercounts in the female population above age 30 (and apparently at even younger ages in the 1880 census). The Census of 1880 was the first providing age by single years for the native population.

Under-Enumeration at Particular Ages for Each Sex

The system of "backward projection" just described gives several estimates of births in a given year. The estimates would agree closely if the completeness of enumeration of each birth class were approximately the same each time it was enumerated. Actually, the estimates based on female children and females above age 30 (in all censuses up to 1950) are exceeded by the estimates based on females enumerated in the age-span 15–29. Estimates based on males show few systematic differences for the age-range 5–59, but births estimated from enumerated males are slightly fewer than the estimates derived from females enumerated at ages 15 to 29.

These differences imply that females aged 15 to 29 have been typically the most fully enumerated group, and that younger and older females have been typically undercounted (the older females by a substantial degree in the earlier censuses), while males 5–59 have been typically undercounted relative to the enumeration of females 15 to 29.

The first estimates of births were therefore obtained by "projecting backward" the native white female population aged 15 to 29, and the native white male population 5 to 59. All estimates derived from counts of the male population were adjusted upward by 3 per cent—the difference between *all* births from 1851 to 1934 based on females 15–29 and males 5–59. The upward adjusted estimates based on males and the estimates based on the females were then averaged. This procedure is equivalent to an assumption that females 15–29 have on the average been fully enumerated, and males 5–59 have on the average been subject to an undercount of 3 per cent. Actually, there is ample evidence that females 15–29 have been slightly undercounted. As will be noted below, the final estimates of births made an allowance for this slight undercount.

Estimates of the Native White Population by Sex and Single-Years of Age, 1880–1950

The birth estimates are an average of several enumerations of a given birth class, each such enumeration increased by the deaths estimated to have occurred between birth and the date of enumeration. The enumerations accepted as usable were for females aged 15–29, and for males 5–59 (adjusted upward by 3 per cent). Once the birth estimates had been calculated, they provided the basis for estimating, quite easily, a consistent set of age–sex distributions of the native population in each census year. All that was required was to project each birth estimate *forward*, using the same estimated proportions surviving that were used for the backward projections. The result is a single-year age-sex distribution consistent with the estimated birth series, adjusted for age heaping and under-enumeration. More accurately, we should say that the estimated populations are adjusted to the average completeness of enumeration of females 15–29. If this group is itself subject to an x per cent undercount, then x per cent should be added to all birth estimates and to every estimate of under-enumeration[3] (except for ages 0–14 in 1950 and 0–4 in 1940, since the "expected populations" for these ages are based on registered births).

Estimates of the Total White Population by Age and Sex, 1880–1950

Estimates of the total white population were obtained by adjusting the enumerated *total* white population by the per cent of under-enumeration estimated by age and sex for the *native* white population. These estimates extend only to age 29 in 1880, 39 in 1890, etc., to 98 in 1950 because, for reasons given earlier, it was not possible to estimate births prior to 1851.[4] For the purpose of estimating completeness of enumeration of the whole population, undercounts for age-groups born before 1851 were assumed equal to those calculated for the same age-sex group in the first census for which such estimates exist. Thus for this purpose the undercounts at ages 30–34 and 35–39 in 1880 were assumed equal to those of 1890, at 40–44 and 45–49 equal to those of 1900, etc.[5] In estimating birth rates 1850–1880, estimates of under-enumeration in the censuses of 1850, 1860, and 1870 were required. Under-enumeration in these censuses was assumed equal, for this purpose, to the total undercount (by sex) in 1880.[6]

---

[3] In fact, there is evidence that females in this age range are undercounted by at least 1.4 per cent. This evidence is discussed below (pp. 13 and 14).

[4] The year 1851 was the first for which it was possible to estimate calendar-year births (and April–March births used in estimating under-enumeration in the 1910, 1930, 1940, and 1950 censuses). It was possible, however, to estimate births for June 1850–May 1851. This estimate was useful for the 1880, 1890, and 1900 censuses. The difference in the day of the year in which the census was taken explains why the estimates of under-enumeration terminate with ages ending in 9 for the early censuses (taken as of June 1), and ages ending in 8 for the later censuses.

[5] Because of the problem cited in the preceding footnote, the estimates of under-enumeration in the 1910 census extended only to age 58. As a result, the undercounts at ages 50–54 in 1880 were assumed equal to those of 1910 and at ages 55–59 equal to those of 1920. Since the same procedure was followed for each census, the "defective births" mentioned in footnote 1, this chapter, have not been of much importance in estimating total undercounts; this is especially true of the later censuses.

[6] The 1870 census, taken during the Reconstruction, was notably deficient, especially in the former Confederate States. After the 1880 census, the Bureau of the Census prepared a revised 1870 figure, based on approximately equal rates of decade growth, from 1860 to 1870 and from 1870 to 1880. This revised figure is the one that was adjusted for under-enumeration.

ALLOWANCE FOR UNDERCOUNTING OF FEMALES AGED 15–29

As mentioned above, there is some evidence to indicate that females 15–29 are in fact undercounted, rather than completely enumerated. The lines of evidence on which this inference is based are:

1. A comparison of our birth estimates with those of Whelpton over the years 1909–1934.[7] Whelpton's estimates are consistently higher, the amount and degree of difference varying from year to year but averaging about 3.6 per cent over the total span. The birth estimates for 1909–1934 are based partly on the enumerated females aged 15–29 in the 1930, 1940, and 1950 censuses. If Whelpton's birth estimates for this period were accepted as valid, it would appear that the average undercount of these females was about 3.6 per cent instead of zero, the undercount we have assumed.

2. A comparison of our estimate of the undercount for native white females aged 15–54 with the estimate of the 1950 census Post-Enumeration Survey for white females of the same ages.[8] Our estimates of the native white female population aged 15–54 in 1950 depend on the assumption of no average undercount at ages 15–29 in 1920, 1930, and 1940 as well as in 1950. This assumption leads to the appearance of a net *overcount* of 0.4 per cent in 1950. However, the P.E.S. estimated an *undercount* of white females in this age range of 1.0 per cent.

3. A comparison of the 1960 enumerated white female population up to age 25 with estimates based on births adjusted for under-registration, registered mortality, and estimated net migration. This comparison showed an undercount of white females at ages 15–24 of 2.3 per cent.

In view of this evidence, it appears plausible to substitute an assumption of a net undercount in each census of females aged 15–29 in place of the assumption that this group is completely enumerated. The conservative estimate we have employed is that the P.E.S. of the 1950 census provided complete coverage

[7] U.S. National Office of Vital Statistics, "Births and Birth Rates in the Entire United States 1909–1948," *Vital Statistics—Special Reports*, Vol. 33, No. 8 (1950).

[8] U.S., Bureau of the Census, *The Post-Enumeration Survey: 1950* (Bureau of the Census, Technical Paper No. 4 [Washington, D.C., 1960]).

of females 15–54, and that our preliminary birth estimates based on the assumption of complete enumeration of females 15–29 in recent censuses are therefore 1.4 per cent too low. (Our preliminary estimates showed a 0.4 per cent overcount of native white females 15–54, while the P.E.S. showed an *undercount* of 1.0 per cent for white females in this age group.) Actually, there are clear indications that the P.E.S. underestimated the undercount of various segments of the population, and it is quite likely that omissions of females 15–54 in 1950 exceeded 1.0 per cent. The figures shown in the various tables include this upward adjustment of 1.4 per cent.

BIRTHS ESTIMATED BY BACKWARD PROJECTION COMPARED WITH BIRTHS CALCULATED FROM REGISTRATIONS

In 1933 the Birth Registration Area was extended to the 48th state, and the nominal coverage, at least, of birth registration became complete. However, it was generally known that not all births were registered and in the censuses of 1940 and 1950 special matching studies were conducted to determine the completeness of birth registration.[9] Omission rates of various categories of births (classified by state, race, and type of attendance, i.e., attended by a physician in a hospital, by a physician at home, by a midwife, or unattended) were determined, and since the composition of births by category is known for each year, it has been possible to adjust for under-registration the recorded number of births for each year since 1935.[10] These birth data since that year provide an opportunity to test the accuracy of the estimates we have prepared by backward projection of census data. Unfortunately, the test is far from representative, for reasons that follow. The reverse projections in general are based on females aged 15–29 and males 5–59, and the final estimate of births for a given year is an average of several figures. Following our standard procedure, we can estimate births for 1935–44 from males 5–14 in 1950, adjusted for an average 3 per cent under-

[9] Sam Shapiro and Joseph Schacter, "Methodology and summary results of the 1950 birth registration test in the United States," *Estadistica*, Vol. X, No. 37, (December 1952) pp. 688–699.

[10] U.S. Department of Health, Education and Welfare, Public Health Service, National Office of Vital Statistics, *Vital Statistics of the United States*, 1959, Vol. I, United States Government Printing Office, pp. 3-1 to 3-35.

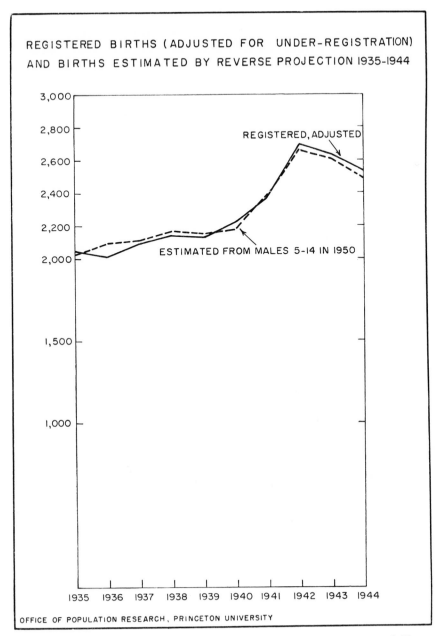

REGISTERED BIRTHS (ADJUSTED FOR UNDER-REGISTRATION)
AND BIRTHS ESTIMATED BY REVERSE PROJECTION 1935-1944

REGISTERED, ADJUSTED

ESTIMATED FROM MALES 5-14 IN 1950

OFFICE OF POPULATION RESEARCH, PRINCETON UNIVERSITY

FIGURE 2. Total White Births in the United States, April–April for each Year 1935–44. Estimated from Registrations Adjusted for Incompleteness, and from Reverse Projections of Males 5–14 in 1950.

count. Data from 1960 could not be employed because the needed tabulations (single-year native white) were not available at the time of writing, and because the adjustment for age heaping would not apply to the 1960 census, where age was determined by responses to a question about date of birth. In sum, the births estimated by reverse projection for 1935–44 cannot be considered typical of earlier estimates. Estimated births for 1935–1944 are compared with adjusted registered data in Figure 2. The agreement is gratifyingly close.

ESTIMATED BIRTH RATES AND FERTILITY RATES

The birth rates presented in Chapters 3 and 4 are obtained by relating estimated annual births to estimates of the annual total white population. Total fertility rates are estimated by a method described in Chapter 6, dependent on estimates of the annual number of females aged 20–39. Annual estimates of the total white population were determined by assuming a constant annual rate of growth within each decade. Estimates of the annual number of white females 20–39 were reached in three different ways. Enumerated females 20–39 in the 1850 and 1860 censuses were adjusted by the undercounts for females of these ages in the 1880 census; annual figures were determined by interpolating between these three censuses.[11] From 1880 to 1900, annual figures were estimated by interpolating along the "diagonal," i.e., estimating the number 20–39 in 1895, for example, as equal to the average of those 15–34 in 1890 and those 25–44 in 1900. From 1900 on, there are estimates of the annual July 1 white population, by age and sex, prepared by the Bureau of the Census. These estimates were increased to account for the under-enumeration of females 20–39 in each census.

ADJUSTING 1900–1950 MORTALITY RATES FOR
UNDER-ENUMERATION

Our original estimates of census enumeration errors imply that the mortality estimates we used in our projections for the period 1900–1950 are in error, mainly in the direction of over-

[11] In preparing these annual estimates of females aged 20–39, it was not possible to use the 1870 census. The revised figure for this census, referred to in footnote 6, this chapter, was for the total white population.

stating mortality (and therefore understating survivorship). We have therefore adjusted the life tables by the estimated errors and used the revised mortality estimates to prepare an alternative set of census enumeration errors. The procedure followed was to calculate the percentage difference in survivorship, for appropriate cohorts, between the adjusted (for errors in enumeration) and unadjusted life tables. The alternative estimates are presented in Tables 21 and 22.

PART II

PRINCIPAL RESULTS:
ANNUAL WHITE BIRTHS AND BIRTH RATES;
THE LONG-TERM TREND IN FERTILITY;
COMPLETENESS OF ENUMERATION

Chapter 3. White Births and Birth Rates in the United States since 1855

White births and birth rates (per 1,000 white persons) in the United States for each year, 1855 to 1960, are shown in Table 1 and Figure 3. Before 1934 the birth estimates are based on our own calculations and are published here for the first time. From 1935 to 1960 the data on births are official figures (adjusted for under-registration by the National Office of Vital Statistics). In every year the base population has been adjusted for census undercounts, so that the birth rates presented here for recent years are lower than official figures, where no such adjustment is made.

TABLE 1
Total Population, Number of Births, and Birth Rates for the
White Population, 1855–1960
(000's Omitted—Rounded to Three Figures)

Year	Total Population	Number of Births[a]	Birth Rate[b]
1855	24,400	1,040	42.8
1856	25,200	1,070	42.5
1857	26,000	1,120	42.8
1858	26,900	1,140	42.5
1859	27,800	1,160	41.8
1860	28,700	1,200	41.8
1861	29,400	1,200	40.9
1862	30,100	1,150	38.2
1863	30,800	1,090	35.4
1864	31,600	1,090	34.6
1865	32,400	1,140	35.4
1866	33,200	1,210	36.6
1867	34,000	1,270	37.4
1868	34,800	1,290	37.1
1869	35,700	1,330	37.3
1870	36,600	1,360	37.1
1871	37,400	1,390	37.2
1872	38,300	1,430	37.4
1873	39,200	1,450	37.1
1874	40,200	1,480	36.8
1875	41,100	1,510	36.8
1876	42,100	1,510	36.0
1877	43,100	1,510	35.2
1878	44,100	1,500	34.1
1879	45,100	1,520	33.6

(CONTINUED)

TABLE 1 (CONTINUED)

Year	Total Population	Number of Births[a]	Birth Rate[b]
1880	46,200	1,550	33.6
1881	47,300	1,600	33.8
1882	48,500	1,630	33.5
1883	49,700	1,680	33.8
1884	50,900	1,720	33.7
1885	52,100	1,740	33.3
1886	53,400	1,740	32.5
1887	54,700	1,760	32.2
1888	56,000	1,810	32.3
1889	57,400	1,840	32.0
1890	58,800	1,830	31.2
1891	59,900	1,900	31.6
1892	61,100	1,970	32.3
1893	62,300	1,990	31.9
1894	63,500	1,980	31.2
1895	64,700	1,990	30.8
1896	66,000	1,990	30.2
1897	67,200	1,960	29.1
1898	68,500	1,960	28.6
1899	69,900	1,980	28.3
1900	71,200	2,030	28.5
1901	72,800	1,960	26.9
1902	74,200	2,000	26.9
1903	75,700	2,060	27.2
1904	77,200	2,120	27.4
1905	78,800	2,200	27.9
1906	80,400	2,260	28.2
1907	82,000	2,300	28.1
1908	83,600	2,340	28.0
1909	85,300	2,360	27.6
1910	86,900	2,380	27.3
1911	88,200	2,360	26.8
1912	89,600	2,410	26.9
1913	91,000	2,450	26.9
1914	92,400	2,460	26.6
1915	93,800	2,460	26.2
1916	95,200	2,490	26.1
1917	96,700	2,550	26.4
1918	98,200	2,540	25.9
1919	99,700	2,360	23.6
1920	101,000	2,530	25.0
1921	103,000	2,620	25.5
1922	104,000	2,440	23.5
1923	105,000	2,460	23.3
1924	107,000	2,500	23.5

(CONTINUED)

TABLE 1 (CONCLUDED)

Year	Total Population	Number of Births[a]	Birth Rate[b]
1925	108,000	2,430	22.4
1926	110,000	2,360	21.5
1927	111,000	2,380	21.4
1928	113,000	2,310	20.5
1929	114,000	2,220	19.4
1930	116,000	2,240	19.4
1931	116,000	2,130	18.3
1932	117,000	2,050	17.5
1933	118,000	1,960	16.7
1934	119,000	2,050	17.3
1935	119,000	2,040	17.1
1936	120,000	2,030	16.9
1937	121,000	2,070	17.1
1938	122,000	2,150	17.6
1939	123,000	2,120	17.3
1940	124,000	2,200	17.8
1941	125,000	2,330	18.6
1942	126,000	2,600	20.6
1943	128,000	2,700	21.1
1944	129,000	2,540	19.7
1945	131,000	2,470	18.9
1946	133,000	2,990	22.6
1947	134,000	3,350	25.0
1948	136,000	3,140	23.1
1949	137,000	3,140	22.8
1950	139,000	3,110	22.4
1951	141,000	3,280	23.2
1952	143,000	3,360	23.4
1953	146,000	3,390	23.3
1954	148,000	3,480	23.5
1955	150,000	3,490	23.2
1956	153,000	3,570	23.4
1957	155,000	3,650	23.5
1958	157,000	3,600	22.9
1959	160,000	3,620	22.6
1960	162,000	3,610	22.2

[a] 1855–1934, original estimates; 1935–1959, registered births adjusted for underregistration; 1960, partly estimated.

[b] Differences between birth rates shown and those that would result from dividing the number of births by the population are due to rounding.

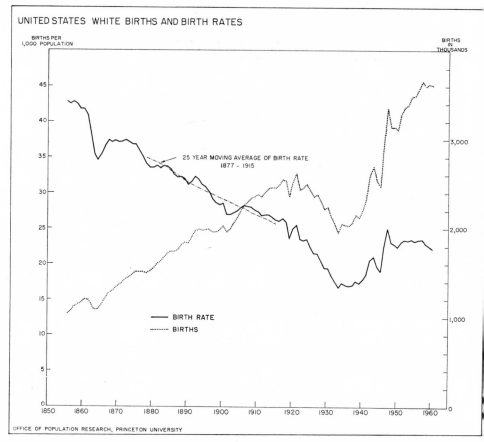

FIGURE 3.   United States White Births and Birth Rates, 1855–1960.
Source: Table 1.

The dominant features of these data are: a steady increase in *numbers* of births to a peak in 1921, followed by a decline and then an increase resumed in the mid-1930's and second, a steady decline in the birth *rate* to a minimum in the 1930's, followed by a sustained recovery. The long-term trend in the birth rate is the subject of Chapter 4. In this chapter the emphasis is on the annual figures, especially annual variations from the trend.

BIRTH DEFICITS IN WARTIME

A distinct trough in the birth rate sequence is evident during the Civil War. The magnitude of the reduction in births caused by the war can be estimated roughly by assuming that "normal" births would have followed a straight-line trend. If a straight line is drawn from the births of 1860 to those of 1873 (the regular down-trend began anew about 1873) the apparent deficit is 944,000 births—6.3 per cent of the total from 1861 to 1872. The deficit during 1862–66 was 500,000–700,000 births, on the assumption, respectively, that normal births can be estimated from a straight line 1860 to 1867, or 1860 to 1873. The loss is from 8 to 10 per cent of the "normal" births during this five-year period.

A definite deficit in births, apparently associated with World War I, occurred in 1919, amounting to about 80 thousand, or some 3.4 per cent of that year's normal births. During World War II the birth rate *increased* until 1943. It then fell off in 1944 and 1945 as full mobilization was reached. If "normal" births for these two years are estimated by a straight line from 1943 to 1946, the two-year deficit amounted to 680,000, or about 13 per cent of the estimated normal. After each World War demobilization was accompanied by birth rates well above the trend, largely compensating for the wartime deficits. No such compensating surplus followed the Civil War.

PEACETIME FLUCTUATIONS IN THE BIRTH RATE, 1870–1915

Although the general downward trend in the birth rate from 1855 to 1934 was approximately linear, there are deviations of substantial magnitude in the annual figures, even in peacetime. Figure 3 includes a 25-term moving average of the birth rate, which indicates a very nearly linear downward trend. Fluctuations about the trend are evident. A simple comparison of annual fluctuations in births and annual fluctuations in business activity does not reveal any conspicuous synchronous or lagging relationship between the two prior to 1914.[1] Perhaps further research will reveal significant interrelations. We have deferred such research, feeling that perhaps it should be conducted by persons

[1] Short-term birth rate fluctuations are, however, strongly correlated with short-term business fluctuations since World War I. See V. L. Galbraith, and D. S. Thomas, "Birth Rates and the Interwar Business Cycles," *Journal of the American Statistical Association*, Vol. XXXVI, No. 216, pp. 465–476; Dudley Kirk, "The Influence of Business Cycles on Marriage and Birth Rates," *Demographic and Economic Change in Developed Countries* (National Bureau of Economic Research, [Princeton, N.J.: Princeton University Press, 1960]), pp. 241–256.

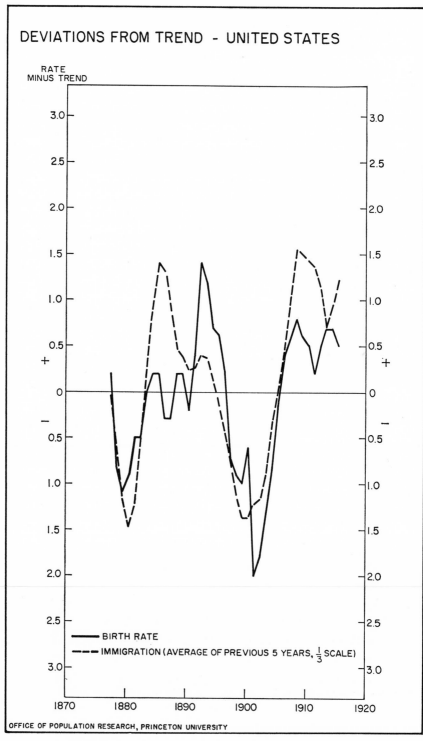

FIGURE 4.   Deviations of United States White Birth Rates
and Immigration Rates from 25-year Moving Average.

familiar with the strong and weak points of the pertinent economic data.

In accord with an idea suggested in a recent article by Easterlin[2] we examined the relationship between fluctuations in immigration and fluctuations in the birth rate. Our hypothesis was that an increase in the foreign-born component in the young childbearing ages would increase the birth rate. This proportion in turn varies in response to fluctuations in the immigration rate during the immediately preceding years. Figure 4 shows deviations of the birth rate and of the immigration rate from 25-year moving averages of each variable. The immigration data are averages of deviations for the five years preceding the date of each birth figure. The correspondence between the deviations is strong enough to confirm a causal connection, although far from sufficient to explain all of the variation in birth rates. Upswings in immigration rates seem to exceed those in birth rates, and the two and one-half-year lag implicit in taking an average of five preceding immigration rates seems sometimes appropriate and sometimes too little. It is the availability of single-year data relating to births that makes it possible for the first time to test this hypothesis, and others which will doubtless prove more fruitful.

Comparison of United States and Australian Birth Rates, 1860–1960

The territories that now form the Commonwealth of Australia kept records of registered births beginning in 1860. For many years (though perhaps not in the early territorial period) Australian demographic data have been of high quality. Because of obvious similarities in the Australian and American societies, we thought it of interest to compare the evolution of the birth rate in the two populations since 1860 (Figure 5). The similarity is startling. Since 1917, the two birth rates have rarely differed by more than one point (one birth per 1,000 persons). In fact, the only exceptions are during World War II. Australia was at war from 1939, and in 1942 and 1943, when American mobilization was still building up, it is not surprising to find the American birth rate higher. By 1944 and 1945, on the other hand, when

---

[2] R. A. Easterlin, "The American Baby Boom in Historical Perspective," *American Economic Review*, Vol. LI, No. 5 (December, 1961), pp. 869–911.

UNITED STATES AND AUSTRALIAN BIRTH RATES

BIRTHS PER
1,000 POPULATION

——— UNITED STATES
·············· AUSTRALIA

YEAR

OFFICE OF POPULATION RESEARCH, PRINCETON UNIVERSITY

FIGURE 5. United States White Birth Rates
and Australian Birth Rates, 1860–1960.

there were more than ten million American men in the armed services, with some six to seven million of these on duty outside the country,[3] Australia had its expatriate service men offset by the large number of Americans serving in Australia.

The large differences for the years between 1861–1872 support our earlier statements about the effect of the American Civil War. There remain the different patterns of fluctuations in the two countries between 1870 and 1915. These are shown more

[3] U.S. Bureau of the Census, "Estimates of the Population of the United States and of the Components of Change, by Age, Color, and Sex: 1940 to 1950," prepared by R. A. Hornseth, *Current Population Reports*, P-25, No. 98 (1954).

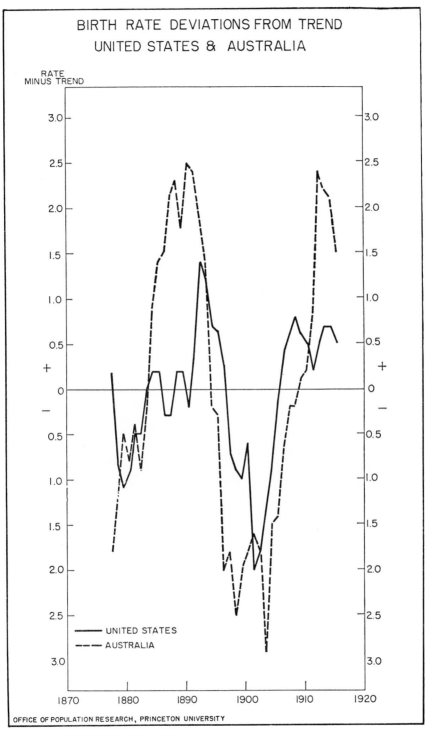

FIGURE 6.   United States White Birth Rates and Australian
Birth Rates as Deviations from 25-Year Moving Average.

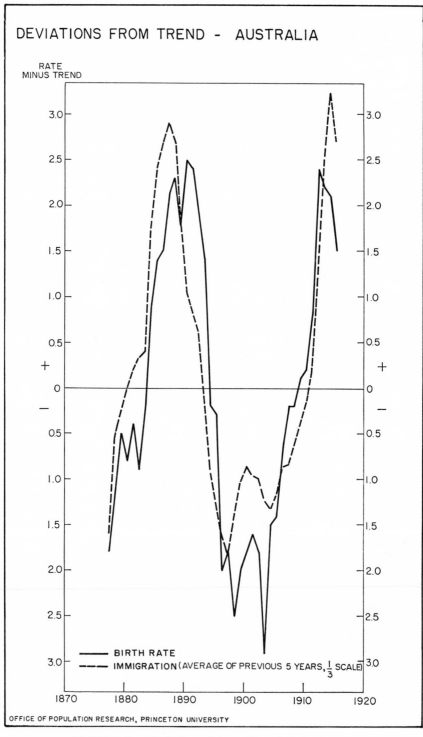

FIGURE 7.   Deviations of Australian Birth Rates and
Immigration Rates from 25-Year Moving Average.

distinctly in Figure 6 where Australian and American birth rates are plotted as deviations from 25-term moving averages.

The deviations are often approximately synchronous, although conspicuously out-of-phase before 1880. The height and width of successive plus and minus swings are only roughly similar. The agreement between the two sets of birth rate deviations is not as close as between the United States birth rate and the lagged United States immigration rates.[4]

Why were the swings in the Australian birth rate different? A partial answer is supplied by Figure 7, showing deviations from the Australian birth-rate trend, and five-term lagged moving averages of deviations from the net-immigration rate trend. The fit is better than in the United States data.[5] Moreover, the relationship between the two curves has the same idiosyncracies as in the United States: upswings in migration exceeding those in the birth rate, and a diminishing "lead" in the immigration series with the passage of time. Though the case is not wholly conclusive, it appears quite strong: basic trends and even variations from trends in the Australian and American birth rates have been remarkably similar, and, in fact, nearly identical since 1917. Some of the differences that occur can be accounted for by particular wartime influences, and others by the effects of the different time-patterns of migration into the two countries.

---

[4] The Pearsonian correlations, over the years 1877–1915, are: between the U.S. and Australian birth rate deviations, 0.61; between the U.S. birth rate and the lagged U.S. immigration data, 0.74.

[5] The correlation of the Australian data is 0.84.

Chapter 4. Long-Term Fertility Trends in the United States Compared to Those in Selected European Countries

The major new information about natality in the United States provided in this book is set forth in Chapter 3 in the form of hitherto unavailable annual data on white births. The general downward trend of the birth rate indicated by these estimates differs little from the trend previously estimated by Thompson and Whelpton.[1] They based their estimates on the population aged 0–4 enumerated in each census, an adjustment for the undercounting of this age group, and estimated survivorship derived from life tables (United States life tables after 1900, and Massachusetts life tables for the nineteenth century). Figure 8 shows our estimates for 1855–1934 and the Thompson-Whelpton estimates for 1860–1930. In the nineteenth century their estimates are for five-year intervals centered on census years, while their estimates for 1910 to 1930 are for single years.

Although the two trends are generally similar, ours usually shows a slightly lower birth rate.[2] Actually, the number of births estimated by Thompson and Whelpton is typically somewhat less than in our series, but our birth rates are lower because we adjusted the census population figures—the denominators of the birth rates—for undercounting.

As Figure 8 shows, our estimates of births and birth rates provide little new information about the general downward trend of fertility that characterized some 130 years of United States history. However, a new perspective on United States trends is gained by a comparison with trends in other countries where the

[1] Warren S. Thompson, and P. K. Whelpton, *Population Trends in the United States* (New York: McGraw-Hill, 1933), p. 263.

[2] The fact that the estimates are unusually far apart around 1890 and unusually close in 1900 can be explained by peculiar features of the enumeration of the child population in those two censuses. Age in 1890 was asked to the nearest birthday, so that (to the degree that instructions were followed in responses) the population tabulated at ages 0–4 was under $4\frac{1}{2}$ rather than under age 5—hence the relatively low Thompson-Whelpton figure for 1890. In 1900 the age question was supplemented by a question about date of birth; the consequent more accurate reporting probably prevented some age overstatement for children 0–4, and resulted in a completeness of enumeration above trend for this age group, accounting for a relatively high figure for 1900 in the Thompson-Whelpton series. In fact, the undercount we estimate for the 0–4 group in 1900 *is* substantially less than trend—less than the estimated undercount in 1910, and no greater than in 1920.

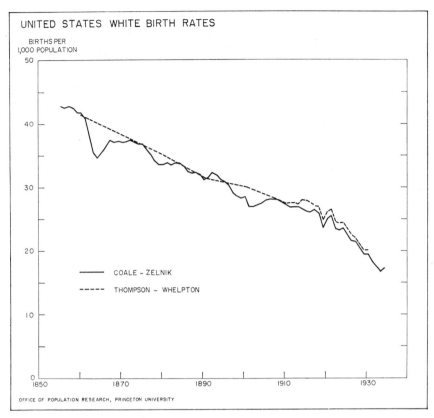

FIGURE 8.   United States White Birth Rates—Coale-Zelnik,
1855–1934 and Thompson-Whelpton, 1860–1930.

birth rate has declined substantially. In Chapter 3 the remarkably close correspondence since 1860 of birth rates in the United States and Australia was noted. In this chapter we shall compare long-term United States experience with that of several European populations.

TRENDS IN THE BIRTH RATE OF THE UNITED STATES AND CERTAIN EUROPEAN COUNTRIES

Figure 9 shows the course of the crude birth rate of the white population of the United States from 1800 to 1934,[3] and corresponding trends in Austria, Great Britain, France, Hungary, Italy, Spain, and Sweden. A striking feature of these trends is

[3] Thompson-Whelpton estimates 1800–1850; Coale-Zelnik, 1855–1934.

33

that only in France and the United States was there a strong and consistent decline in the early part of the nineteenth century. Each of the other countries experienced a sustained decline in the birth rate, that began after the middle of the nineteenth century,

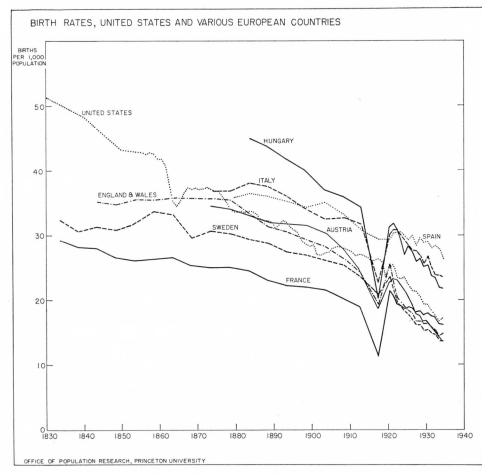

FIGURE 9.   Birth Rates, 1830–1934, for United States
White Population and Various European Countries.

but in no instance later than the 1880's. The nineteenth century "plateau" characteristic of all but France and the United States was at levels ranging from nearly 45 per thousand in Hungary to about 33 in Sweden. France apparently experienced a falling birth rate as early as about 1770, from a level somewhere between the nineteenth century "plateaus" of Austria and Great Britain.

The birth rate in the United States at the beginning of the nineteenth century was markedly higher than that ever recorded for any European country and is equalled in reliably recorded data only by such unusually fertile populations as the Hutterites[4] and the inhabitants of the Cocos-Keeling Islands.[5]

By the 1850's the declining United States birth rate had fallen below that of Hungary; by 1870 below Austria; and by 1880 below Italy and Spain. Also, by 1880 the United States had reduced its birth rate to the level then current in Great Britain, and nearly to Sweden's level. From 1880 until 1940 the most conspicuous feature of the trends is their roughly parallel course in all of the countries except France and Sweden which, having already achieved a moderate level, were declining more slowly. From 1880 to 1930 the greatest decline was 19.6 per thousand (Hungary) and the least (France excluded) was 7.5 (Spain).

The various time patterns of declining birth rates makes any universally applicable and simple explanation difficult to find. The birth rate in the United States fell extensively—from 55 to 41 per thousand—between 1800 and 1860, while the population remained nearly 80 per cent rural. Late nineteenth century declines began at about the same time (i.e., the 1880's) in Great Britain, the pioneer in industrialization and highly industrialized by then, and in Hungary and Spain, not usually considered industrial leaders.

The kinds of social and economic changes that led to lower birth rates appear to have been more diverse than mere differences in the "starting dates" and rapidity of industrialization or observed differences in the forms of modernization accompanying industrialization. There appears to be no instance of the development of a highly industrialized economy without a major decline in the birth rate, but France, the United States, and several European countries provide instances of falling birth rates in the absence of marked industrialization. To account for the decline in fertility in non-industrial environments would be a fruitful form of historical research.

[4] J. W. Eaton, and A. J. Mayer, "The Social Biology of Very High Fertility Among the Hutterites," *Human Biology*, September, 1953, No. 3, pp. 206–264.

[5] T. E. Smith, "The Cocos-Keeling Islands: A Demographic Laboratory," *Population Studies*, November, 1960, No. 2, pp. 94–130.

TABLE 2
Total Fertility Rates for the White Population, 1800–1960[a]

Year	Total Fertility Rate	Year	Total Fertility Rate	Year	Total Fertility Rate
1800	7.04	1886	4.11	1923	2.96
1810	6.92	1887	4.06	1924	2.98
1820	6.73	1888	4.06	1925	2.84
1830	6.55	1889	3.99	1926	2.73
1840	6.14			1927	2.72
1850	5.42	1890	3.87	1928	2.60
		1891	3.93	1929	2.46
1855	5.31	1892	4.01		
1856	5.26	1893	3.98	1930	2.45
1857	5.30	1894	3.89	1931	2.31
1858	5.30	1895	3.83	1932	2.22
1859	5.21	1896	3.77	1933	2.11
1860	5.21	1897	3.64	1934	2.19
1861	5.07	1898	3.60	1935	2.14
1862	4.72	1899	3.57	1936	2.10
1863	4.38			1937	2.12
1864	4.26	1900	3.56	1938	2.18
		1901	3.38	1939	2.13
1865	4.34	1902	3.38		
1866	4.47	1903	3.41	1940	2.19
1867	4.56	1904	3.44	1941	2.29
1868	4.54	1905	3.50	1942	2.54
1869	4.57	1906	3.53	1943	2.63
1870	4.55	1907	3.52	1944	2.48
1871	4.55	1908	3.51	1945	2.40
1872	4.58	1909	3.46	1946	2.88
1873	4.57			1947	3.21
1874	4.54	1910	3.42	1948	3.01
		1911	3.34	1949	3.00
1875	4.55	1912	3.35		
1876	4.45	1913	3.35	1950	2.97
1877	4.37	1914	3.30	1951	3.14
1878	4.27	1915	3.25	1952	3.23
1879	4.23	1916	3.23	1953	3.29
1880	4.24	1917	3.28	1954	3.39
1881	4.28	1918	3.24	1955	3.42
1882	4.25	1919	3.00	1956	3.51
1883	4.29			1957	3.58
1884	4.29	1920	3.17	1958	3.51
		1921	3.24	1959	3.51
1885	4.23	1922	2.97	1960	3.52

[a] The estimation of total fertility rates is by different methods in each of three periods: (1) from 1935 to 1960, when age-specific fertility schedules are available, based on registered births adjusted for under-registration; (2) from 1855 to 1934, when our birth estimates are available; and (3) prior to 1855, when the Thompson-Whelpton estimates of births for five-year intervals centered on census dates are employed. For the most recent period we obtained a figure for total fertility by multiplying the officially calculated Gross Reproduction

A Comparison of Trends in Total Fertility

The *birth rate* is a measure of the fertility of the population as a whole. It reflects such influences as unusually plentiful or sparse proportions of women at the most fertile ages in addition to the number of children each woman bears.

In contrast, the *total fertility rate* is a measure unaffected by such influences as the age distribution, and reflects childbearing performance only. It summarizes the production of births per woman passing through life, rather than the rate of occurrence of births in the whole population. Specifically, total fertility is the average number of children per woman that would be born to a hypothetical group subject at each age to the childbearing rate experienced in the observed population. Thus the total fertility of 2.1 in 1936 among white women in the United States means that women bearing children at 1936 rates would reach menopause having experienced an average of 2.1 births apiece.

We have estimated the course of total fertility in the United States since 1800 (Table 2; Figure 10). During all but the most

---

Rate by one plus the sex ratio at birth for the year in question, and by the ratio $\dfrac{\text{census estimate of women 20–39}}{\text{our estimate of women 20–39}}$. In effect, official data were adjusted for census undercounts of women of childbearing age.

For the earlier periods, we made use of equation (6), p. 71, Chapter 6. It follows from this equation that $F = G(\beta - \alpha)$, provided that there is no correlation between the age distribution and the fertility schedule over the childbearing span. Since the age distribution is approximately linear over the relevant ages prior to 1935, it is possible to insure that this relationship holds by choosing approximate limits (α and β) for the childbearing span such that $\dfrac{\alpha + \beta}{2}$ coincides with the mean age of childbearing. G then is the ratio of births to women in this particular age span. We let $\beta = 40$ years for these computations, and chose α so that $\dfrac{\alpha + \beta}{2}$ equals the estimated mean age of childbearing. If this mean age is $30 - 2.5x$, then the number of women in the approximate age interval is about $_{20}W_{20} + x(_5W_{15})$, where $_nW_x$ is the number of women aged x to $x + n$. The width of this age interval is $20 + 5x$ years. In other words, we constructed our estimates of total fertility from estimated births, the adjusted female age distribution, and the estimated mean age of childbearing. Mean age of childbearing in 1920 and 1930 was obtained from age-specific fertility rates for the Birth Registration Area. Prior to 1920, we estimated the mean age of childbearing from the singulate mean age at marriage, using a regression based on data from seven countries where both pieces of information were available. Singulate mean age at marriage in turn was calculated from intercensal changes in proportions single for 1910 and 1900, and from the proportions single in the 1890 census for 1890. Prior to 1890 we assumed that mean age at marriage increased in a linear fashion from age 20 in 1800.

TOTAL FERTILITY, UNITED STATES WHITE POPULATION

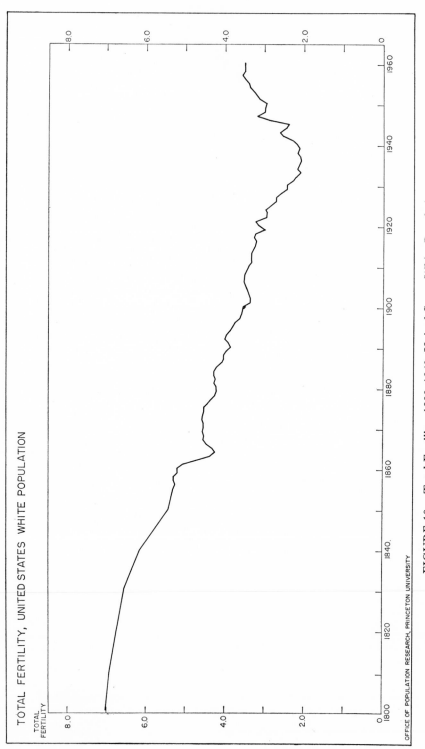

FIGURE 10. Total Fertility, 1800–1960, United States White Population.
Source: Table 2

INDEX OF UNITED STATES WHITE BIRTH RATES AND TOTAL FERTILITY

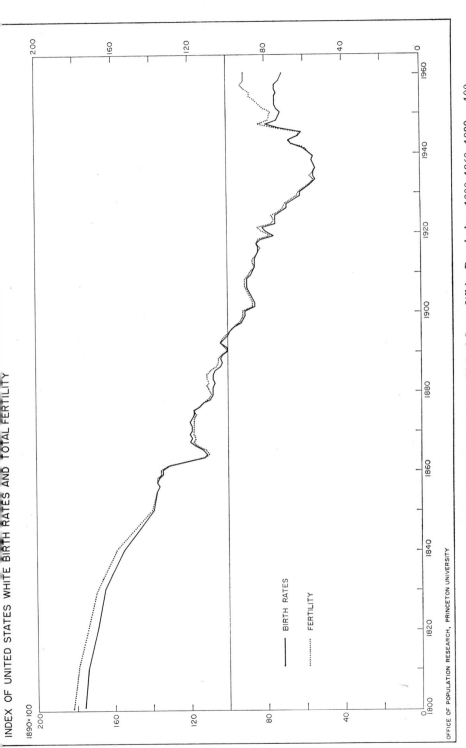

FIGURE 11. Indexes of Birth Rates and Total Fertility, United States White Population, 1800–1960; 1890 = 100.
Source: Computed from Tables 1 and 2

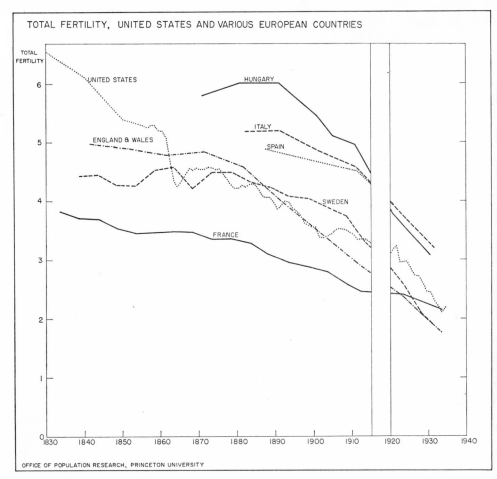

FIGURE 12.   Total Fertility, 1830–1934, for the United States
White Population and Various European Countries.

recent years (i.e., since the late 1940's) the time sequence of the
total fertility rate closely paralleled that of the birth rate (Figure
11). This parallelism implies that the structure of the population
remained about equally favorable to the production of births,
even though the age composition underwent major changes. As
explained in Chapter 6, this relatively constant relation between
the birth rate and total fertility was the result of a fortuitous
combination of offsetting factors. For example, a gradually rising
proportion of women aged 15–44 during the nineteenth century,

which would cause the birth rate to increase relative to total fertility, was to a large extent cancelled by a trend toward later childbearing, which reduces the birth rate relative to total fertility. After 1947 a markedly unfavorable age distribution developed as the small birth classes of the 1930's began to enter the childbearing ages.

During most of the nineteenth century the age structure of the United States population and the prevalent age at marriage were more favorable to a high birth rate than were the conditions then prevailing in European countries. In consequence, total fertility in the United States was lower relative to European fertility than was the United States birth rate relative to European birth rates. This point is evident in a comparison of Figures 9 and 12. By the time the United States had lowered its birth rate to a level about equal to that in England and Wales (in 1880), its total fertility was 9 per cent lower. Even in 1870, when the United States birth rate was 37 per thousand compared to about 36 in England and Wales, total fertility in the United States was lower. An even more striking illustration of divergence between relative total fertility and relative birth rates is afforded by a comparison of Swedish and United States data. Although the United States birth rate has been consistently higher than Sweden's, its total fertility was consistently lower from 1875 until shortly before World War I.

The salient features of United States fertility trends relative to those of European countries are that the birth rate and the total fertility rate in the United States were higher in the early nineteenth century than in most European countries, but that the steady decline in United States fertility brought the birth rate into line, by 1870, with the low levels of Western Europe. Because earlier childbearing and a favorable age structure inflated the United States birth rate in the nineteenth century, total fertility of the United States was lower relative to European experience than was its crude birth rate. In fact, in the late nineteenth century, only France had clearly lower fertility than the United States.

Chapter 5. Estimates of Census Enumeration Errors

A natural by-product of the estimates of white births 1855–1934 presented in Chapter 3 is an appraisal of the accuracy of the reported number of native whites in the decennial censuses from 1880 to 1950. This appraisal is made possible by calculating the number of each annual set of white births expected to survive to the date of each of the decennial censuses in which these survivors were enumerated.

This projection of survivors from estimated numbers born provides a truncated age distribution terminating at age 29 in 1880, and at age 98 seventy years later in 1950.[1] We have extended these estimated undercounts in three ways:

1. The undercount of the total white population for any age-sex-census group was assumed to be the same as that of the comparable native white population. In fact, age heaping and under-enumeration have undoubtedly been somewhat more pronounced among the foreign-born, but since natives constitute a substantial majority of every age-group, the percentage undercounts for the native white population probably did not differ greatly from the undercounts for all whites.

2. Undercounts for age-groups born earlier than our earliest birth estimate were approximated by the estimated undercount from the earliest census in which an estimate for the given age-group is available. Thus we could not estimate directly the undercount at ages 30–34 in 1880, and assumed it to be the same as the undercount at those ages in 1890.

3. It is possible to estimate the expected native white population in 1960, but at the time this book was written, the single-year age distribution of native whites enumerated in the 1960 census was not available. Therefore we have estimated the completeness of enumeration of the *total* white population in 1960, based on our estimates of the 1950 total white population and intercensal estimates of births, deaths, and net migration.

Figures 13 and 14 show the census enumeration errors, by

---

[1] The birth estimates for 1851–1854 were used for estimating expected populations in each of the censuses, even though we did not find the individual estimates sufficiently plausible for publication. Thus estimated errors for the oldest group in each census must be viewed with some skepticism.

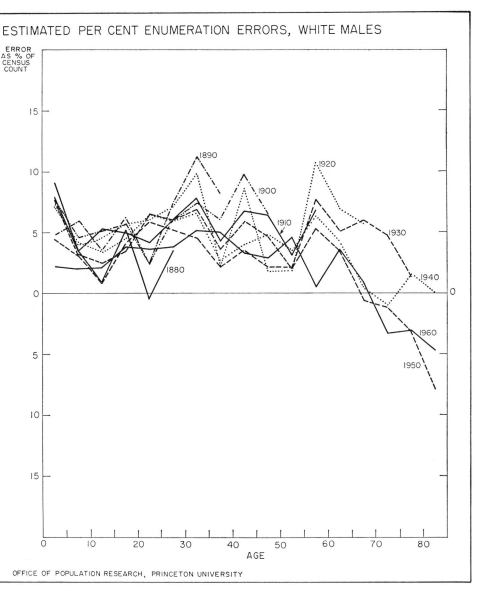

FIGURE 13. Estimated Per Cent Census Enumeration Errors, by Five-Year
Age-Groups, Native White Males, 1880–1950 and Total White Males, 1960.
Source: Tables 14 and 18

43

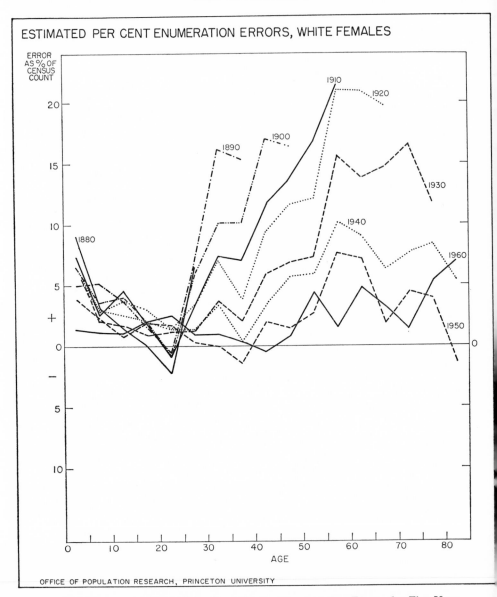

FIGURE 14. Estimated Per Cent Census Enumeration Errors, by Five-Year Age-Groups, Native White Females, 1880–1950 and Total White Females, 1960. Source: Tables 15 and 18

five-year age-groups and by sex, for the native whites in each census from 1880 to 1950 and total whites in 1960. Figure 15 shows these same error rates plotted separately for each age-group over time. It should be borne in mind that these errors represent the net effect, over each five-year age-range, of errors in the reporting of age and errors in the completeness of enumeration. It is impossible to distinguish the contribution of each kind of error.

FEATURES OF THE UNDERCOUNTS

Two censuses (1920 and 1940) show larger undercounts at most of the younger ages than do adjacent censuses. It is a logical inference that defects in organization or field work produced relatively incomplete coverage in these censuses. The 1930 census, in contrast, has generally smaller undercounts at these ages than the 1920 or 1940 census.

When interpreting the time trends shown in Figure 15, the reader should bear in mind our assumption that females aged 15–29 have been subject to an unchanging rate of net undercount (1.4 per cent). Thus at ages up to 20, Figure 15 shows trends that have been irregular for males and females alike, with no consistent tendency for improving or worsening coverage. From a rigorous point of view, these data show that the trend at ages up to 20 has been about parallel to the trend in completeness of enumeration of females 15–29. Note that undercounts among male children and adolescents have been consistently higher than among females.

Above age 25 the most striking feature of the trends in undercounts is the consistent steep decline in rates of under-enumeration in the female population, in contrast to the nearly level, or irregular and gradually declining rates of male under-enumeration. Again, it should be noted that, strictly speaking, these trends are relative to the trend among females aged 15–29.

As can be seen in Figures 14 and 15, the error in some censuses for females 55–64 years of age reaches the remarkable level of 21 per cent. In subsequent sections of this chapter we will re-examine the data and assumptions on which these estimates are based. We will attempt to show (a) that these estimates are conservative, in view of the evidence, and (b) that alternative

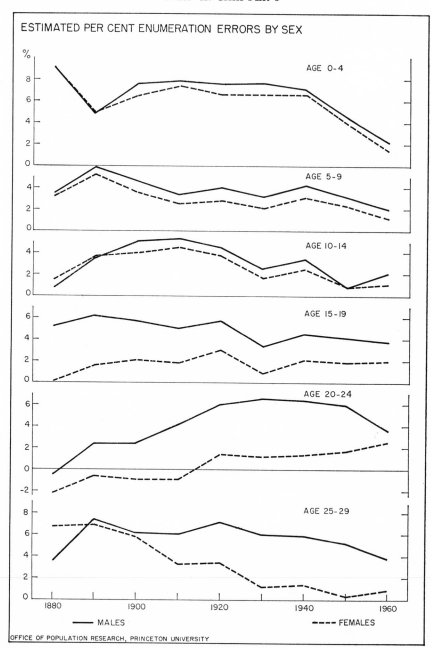

FIGURE 15*a*.   Estimated Per Cent Census Enumeration Errors,
by Age and Sex, for the White Population, 1880–1960.

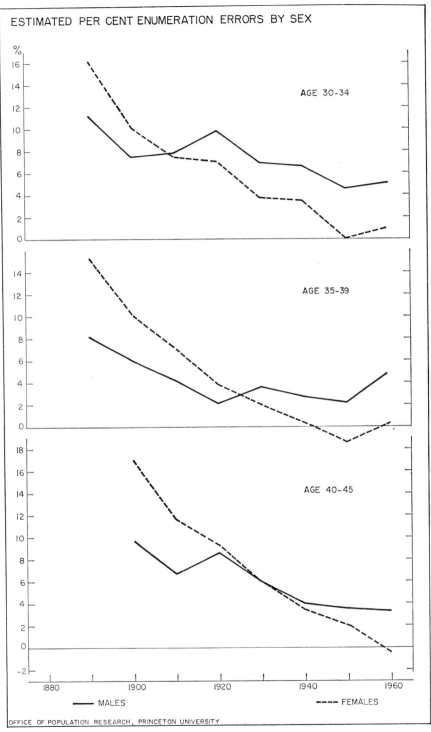

FIGURE 15*b*. Estimated Per Cent Census Enumeration Errors,
by Age and Sex, for the White Population, 1880–1960.

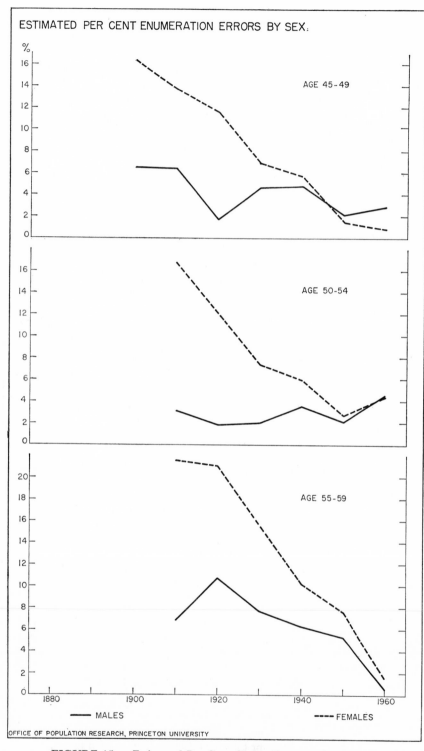

FIGURE 15c. Estimated Per Cent Census Enumeration Errors,
by Age and Sex, for the White Population, 1900–1960.

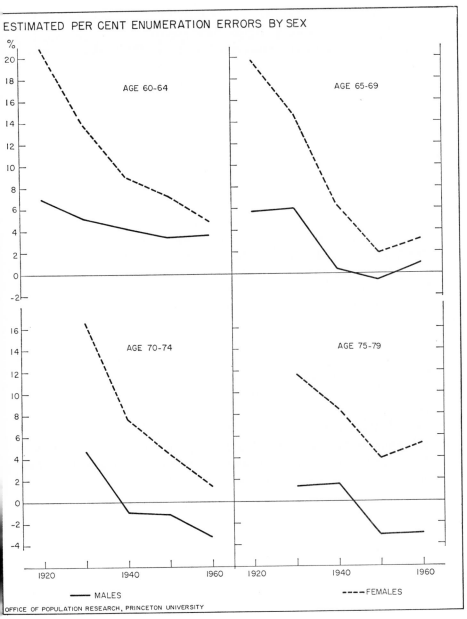

ESTIMATED PER CENT ENUMERATION ERRORS BY SEX

OFFICE OF POPULATION RESEARCH, PRINCETON UNIVERSITY

FIGURE 15*d*.   Estimated Per Cent Census Enumeration Errors,
by Age and Sex, for the White Population, 1920–1960.
Source: Tables 14, 15 and 18

49

explanations or hypotheses to account for these estimates are inconsistent with some parts of the evidence.

A peculiarity in the pattern of errors in 1890 calls for comment. In this census, in contrast to all others, the error for persons 5–9 years old is greater than at 0–4 for both sexes. This reversal is undoubtedly the result of a different age question asked in 1890 ("age at nearest birthday").

In the technical chapter dealing with the adjustments for age heaping, it is noted that no change in the pattern of single-year age heaping was discernible for those ages which would presumably have been affected by the old-age assistance legislation enacted in the 1930's. However, the enumeration errors shown in Figures 13 and 14 do indicate that there was a change in pattern for *five-year* age-groups. In 1930 the error rate for those 60–64 was below the rate for those 65–69. In 1940 and 1950 there was a much greater decrease in the error rate at 65–69 than at 60–64. As a consequence, the error rate at 65–69 dropped below that for 60–64 in both 1940 and 1950. These changes occurred for both males and females.

Some of the decline in the error rate for those aged 65–69 is probably a result of changes in age misreporting. Most of the decline, however, appears to be the result of improvement in the completeness of enumeration of older persons. For both sexes, there is a decline in the error rate for those 60–64 from 1920 through 1950. If the decrease in the error for the 65–69 year olds had been solely the result of a shift in age reporting, then the error rate for the 60–64 year olds should have increased in 1940 and 1950 rather than decreased.

Another feature of the estimated completeness of enumeration of older persons is the appearance in recent censuses of apparent overcounts, especially for males. An obvious explanation of an overcount of older native whites is the possibility that some foreign-born persons were reported as native. However, this possibility is not borne out by the fragmentary available evidence. It is not supported by the information on reporting of nativity contained in the Post-Enumeration Survey for 1950.[2] The 1950 P.E.S. does not provide an age-nativity cross-classifi-

---

[2] U.S., Bureau of the Census, *The Post-Enumeration Survey: 1950* (Bureau of the Census, Technical Paper No. 4 [Washington, D.C., 1960]) Table 2, p. 32.

cation of errors, but one table does give estimates of the error in reporting nativity. This table shows that the error resulting from misclassification of nativity is considerably smaller than the error resulting from incomplete coverage. In fact, this table indicates that more natives were reported as foreign-born in the 1950 census than vice versa.

Additional evidence refuting the argument that the overcounts result from the "passing" of foreign-born as native is provided by our estimates of the errors in 1960 for *total* whites, which show males 70 and over as being overcounted. The 1960 estimates of expected populations are derived from our adjusted 1950 figures and any error introduced by our adjustments to the 1950 data is of course carried forward to our 1960 estimates. However, even if we had used the enumerated 1950 total white population, rather than our adjusted figures, to estimate the 1960 population, we still would have estimated an overcount at the older ages in 1960 for total whites.[3] Although an overcount in natives can result from "passing," this phenomenon cannot explain overcounts in the total population.

We will show, in a later section of this chapter, that some of these overcounts are possibly spurious, perhaps resulting from estimates of survivorship that are too low. Any genuine overcounts at the extreme upper ages are probably the combined result of age overstatement that tends to inflate the number reported at very old ages, and improved coverage from one census to the next of older persons in general. There is a widespread tendency, in the censuses of many countries, for persons at advanced ages to overstate their age. Because the age distribution falls off very rapidly at high ages, a small proportion at a given age reported at an older age substantially inflates the latter group.

Until 1960, men and women aged 55–59 were heavily under-

---

[3] For ages 65 and over in 1950 our adjustments have resulted in an estimated "true" population smaller than the enumerated population. If the apparent overcount of native whites was a result of misclassification of foreign-born as natives, then the size of the enumerated total white population would be more accurate, and we would be projecting forward to 1960 a larger population than the one we have used. As indicated, we would still have estimated overcounts in 1960.

The overcount for males 70–74 in 1960 could certainly not be explained in this way as we have projected forward a larger population 60–64 years of age in 1950 than was enumerated. That is, we estimated an undercount for this group.

counted in every census. In a striking reversal the error rate in 1960 for this age group is quite low and even falls below the error rate for the two adjacent age-groups. Apparently the 1960 census is characterized by "year heaping" rather than age heaping. We believe that the single-year tabulation of the 1960 census will show too many people reported at age 59—the result of selecting, or heaping into, the year 1900 in response to the question "year of birth." We cannot make a definitive test of this assertion because at this time the necessary 1960 tabulations are not available. However, the distribution for Vermont (the one area for which this information is available at the time of writing) shows a strong preference for age 59.

The estimates for 1960 also indicate a relatively uniform error rate, for each sex, for the first three age groups. There appears to have been a substantial decrease in the undercounting at 0–4 and a smaller improvement at 5–9; the result is an approximately equal error rate for 0–4, 5–9, and 10–14. It is possible that undercounts at ages 0–9 in 1960 were underestimated because births occurring during the 1950's to Americans overseas were omitted from the birth register, and also from estimates of under registration. According to figures supplied by the Passport Office, U.S. Department of State, a total of 329,835 such births were reported 1950–1959 to United States consular offices. Allowance for these births increases the estimated undercounts at 0–4 by about 1.1%, and at 5–9 by about .7%. A perplexing question is why males, especially at 0–4, should be undercounted to a greater degree than females. We do not know of an explanation that accounts for this differential. The only plausible hypothesis is that some male children are recorded as female, perhaps because of a false inference from names such as Frances and Marion.

COMPARISON WITH AN EARLIER ESTIMATE OF UNDERCOUNTS

In 1955 Coale calculated estimates of undercounts in the 1950 census by age, sex, and color on the basis of an assumption of similar errors in the 1930, 1940, and 1950 censuses.[4] This as-

---

[4] Ansley J. Coale, "The Population of the United States in 1950 Classified by Age, Sex, and Color—A Revision of Census Figures," *Journal of the American Statistical Association*, Vol. L (March 1955), pp. 16–54.

sumption is different from those underlying the estimates presented here, and it is reassuring to find that the age-pattern of errors (and the general level) is similar (Figure 16).

The most striking difference between the two sets of estimates is that the new male estimates usually have higher error rates, especially at ages 15–29; and yet the new female estimated errors, generally closer to the earlier estimates, are, on the average, lower. In the 1955 estimates, the sexes were calculated independently, while in the estimated errors presented here, consistency between male and female error rates is automatically assured by tying the male and female cohorts through the sex ratio at birth.

IMPLICATIONS OF THE UNDERCOUNTS

Deficiencies in the completeness and accuracy of decennial enumerations may have important consequences for demographic analysis; for example, where *per capita* figures are being calculated. Coale noted that in 1950 registered births were corrected for under-registration, but no correction was introduced to account for under-enumeration of the total population, with the result that: ". . . ironically enough, the preliminary birth rate based on registered births (and the census population) is probably closer to reality than the birth rate based on adjusted birth figures."[5]

Census errors can have a much stronger effect on age-specific rates (where events occurring to persons in specific age-sex groups are divided by the numbers in these groups) because some groups (e.g., older females) have been much more strongly under-enumerated than the whole population. Errors in age-specific rates are especially prominent when the events upon which the rates are based are recorded in a data system independent of the census itself. Then there will be no systematic tendency for compensating errors in numerator and denominator. An example is age-specific mortality rates. There is no reason to suppose that the factors causing the omission of persons with certain characteristics from the census would cause the omission of their deaths from the vital statistics register; nor are age misstatements occurring in the census likely to be precisely duplicated in errors of age on death certificates.

[5] *Ibid.*, p. 47.

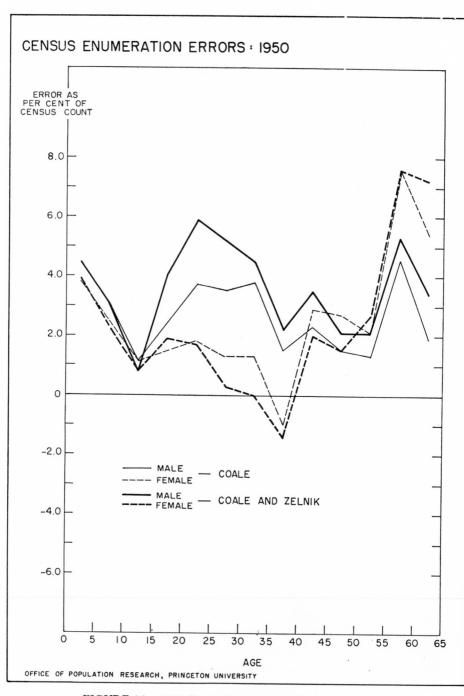

FIGURE 16. 1950 Census Enumeration Errors, by Age and Sex—Coale-Zelnik Estimates and Earlier Coale Estimates.

We have calculated the effect on life tables of the estimated net omissions from the censuses. Life tables are constructed from age-specific mortality rates, where the numerator of each rate is the number of deaths registered in some age-sex group during a period (typically centered on a census year), and the denominator is the number of persons "at risk" in the age-sex group during the period, estimated from a census count. If the number of deaths registered is approximately correct, an undercount of 10 per cent in a particular age-sex group causes an overstatement of 10 per cent in the age-specific mortality rate. The effect on the life table death rate (q_x)—the probability of dying in the age interval—is of about the same magnitude. We have constructed adjusted life tables with mortality rates modified by a correction for under-enumeration of the population in each age-sex group.[6] These adjusted tables have lower mortality rates (and higher survivorship rates) especially in age-groups subject to large undercounts.

The largest undercounts were among older women, especially in the earlier censuses. By 1950 these undercounts had greatly moderated. This development implies that female mortality above age 30, but especially above age 40, was substantially overstated in the 1900 life tables, and that this overstatement diminished in later tables, becoming almost negligible by 1950. Because of the different pattern of male undercounts, the underestimation of male mortality has not been subject to a similarly pronounced trend.

These facts indicate the need to reassess the time trend of sex differentials in mortality. Female mortality rates have fallen much more extensively than male, and the difference between male and female expectation of life at birth in the United States is now one of the largest in the world. The existence of census undercounts implies that some of the widening of sex differentials is spurious. Adjustment for under-enumeration does not narrow the present gap, but indicates that it was wider earlier in the century. In short, the decline in female mortality was more moderate than official data indicate. Tables 3 and 4 list adjusted and unadjusted expectations of life at five-year intervals.[7]

---

[6] See Chapter 9, pp. 154–155 for details.
[7] Other functions for the adjusted life tables (l_x and q_x) are tabulated in Appendix C.

TABLE 3
Life Expectancies ($\mathring{e}_x$'s) for White Males in U.S. Life Tables Adjusted for
Under-Enumeration and Increase Over Unadjusted Life Tables: 1901–1950

Age	1901		1910		1920	
	$\mathring{e}_x$	Increase	$\mathring{e}_x$	Increase	$\mathring{e}_x$	Increase
0–4	48.97	.74	50.94	.71	57.02	.68
5–9	55.35	.92	56.23	.86	59.07	.76
10–14	51.47	.88	52.15	.83	54.90	.75
15–19	47.11	.86	47.71	.80	50.48	.74
20–24	43.04	.85	43.49	.78	46.30	.70
25–29	39.36	.84	39.55	.76	42.25	.65
30–34	35.65	.77	35.58	.71	38.24	.59
35–39	31.99	.70	31.71	.63	34.24	.50
40–44	28.40	.66	28.03	.60	30.35	.49
45–49	24.75	.54	24.39	.53	26.42	.42
50–54	21.24	.48	20.87	.48	22.63	.41
55–59	17.90	.48	17.50	.47	19.02	.43
60–64	14.67	.32	14.31	.33	15.55	.30
65–69	11.74	.23	11.47	.22	12.41	.20
70–74	9.16	.13	8.95	.12	9.63	.08
75–79	6.85	.01	6.75	.00	7.31	.01
80–84	5.05	−.05	5.03	−.06	5.40	−.07
85–89	3.68	−.13	3.75	−.13	3.92	−.14

Life Table

Age	1930		1940		1950	
	$\mathring{e}_x$	Increase	$\mathring{e}_x$	Increase	$\mathring{e}_x$	Increase
0–4	59.68	.56	63.11	.30	66.47	.16
5–9	59.98	.60	62.00	.32	63.93	.16
10–14	55.53	.57	57.33	.30	59.14	.16
15–19	50.97	.58	52.63	.30	54.34	.16
20–24	46.58	.56	48.04	.28	49.65	.13
25–29	42.31	.53	43.54	.26	45.04	.11
30–34	38.03	.49	39.04	.24	40.38	.09
35–39	33.79	.46	34.57	.21	35.74	.06
40–44	29.66	.44	30.23	.20	31.23	.06
45–49	25.67	.39	26.07	.20	26.90	.03
50–54	21.87	.36	22.12	.16	22.85	.02
55–59	18.34	.37	18.47	.13	19.11	.00
60–64	14.99	.27	15.09	.04	15.55	−.21
65–69	11.99	.22	12.05	−.02	12.56	−.19
70–74	9.33	.13	9.40	−.02	9.87	−.20
75–79	7.04	.02	7.18	.01	7.54	−.23
80–84	5.20	−.06	5.31	−.07	5.62	−.26
85–89	3.86	−.13	3.88	−.14	4.21	−.14

TABLE 4

Life Expectancies ($\mathring{e}_x$'s) for White Females in U.S. Life Tables Adjusted for
Under-Enumeration and Increase over Unadjusted Life Tables: 1901–1950

	Life Table					
Age	1901		1910		1920	
	$\mathring{e}_x$	Increase	$\mathring{e}_x$	Increase	$\mathring{e}_x$	Increase
0–4	52.64	1.56	55.05	1.43	59.92	1.39
5–9	57.90	1.87	59.35	1.68	60.95	1.52
10–14	54.02	1.87	55.24	1.67	56.69	1.52
15–19	49.67	1.88	50.76	1.64	52.18	1.51
20–24	45.67	1.90	46.55	1.67	47.97	1.51
25–29	42.03	1.98	42.59	1.71	44.07	1.52
30–34	38.40	1.98	38.69	1.73	40.25	1.53
35–39	34.72	1.90	34.79	1.70	36.36	1.50
40–44	31.00	1.83	30.94	1.68	32.44	1.50
45–49	27.17	1.66	27.06	1.61	28.44	1.46
50–54	23.42	1.53	23.26	1.52	24.50	1.38
55–59	19.79	1.36	19.54	1.36	20.70	1.30
60–64	16.32	1.09	16.03	1.11	16.99	1.06
65–69	13.03	.80	12.78	.81	13.53	.78
70–74	10.18	.59	9.98	.60	10.53	.59
75–79	7.60	.27	7.47	.27	7.88	.26
80–84	5.57	.07	5.43	.08	5.77	.07
85–89	3.98	−.12	3.94	−.12	4.11	−.13

	Life Table					
Age	1930		1940		1950	
	$\mathring{e}_x$	Increase	$\mathring{e}_x$	Increase	e_x	Increase
0–4	63.65	.98	67.86	.57	72.28	.25
5–9	63.23	1.06	66.18	.61	69.34	.25
10–14	58.72	1.07	61.46	.61	64.51	.25
15–19	54.07	1.07	56.68	.61	59.64	.25
20–24	49.61	1.09	52.00	.62	54.82	.26
25–29	45.35	1.10	47.40	.62	50.03	.26
30–34	41.11	1.12	42.84	.63	45.26	.26
35–39	36.87	1.14	38.30	.60	40.54	.26
40–44	32.67	1.15	33.86	.61	35.90	.26
45–49	28.53	1.14	29.51	.61	31.37	.25
50–54	24.51	1.10	25.30	.58	27.00	.24
55–59	20.68	1.08	21.29	.56	22.81	.23
60–64	16.98	.93	17.47	.47	18.80	.16
65–69	13.59	.78	13.95	.39	15.07	.07
70–74	10.56	.58	10.84	.34	11.75	.07
75–79	7.82	.26	8.17	.25	8.88	.01
80–84	5.70	.07	5.95	.07	6.49	−.10
85–89	4.11	−.13	4.21	−.13	4.70	−.13

Survivorship rates adjusted for under-enumeration would modify the estimated undercounts in subsequent censuses. We return to this point later in this chapter (p. 62).

EVALUATION OF THE ASSUMPTION THAT FEMALES AGED 15–29 WERE ALMOST COMPLETELY ENUMERATED

The following facts provide the foundation on which we base the assumption of relatively complete enumeration of women 15–29 years of age:

1. Births estimated by the backward projection of females 15–29 in one census tend to exceed births projected from females 5–14 and over 30 in other censuses. The relative deficiencies in births projected from ages 30 and over are greater, the earlier the census upon which the projection is based.

2. Births projected backward from males 5–59 are reasonably consistent with projections from one census to another, with no strong age-pattern. However, these births average about 3 per cent less than those from females 15–29.

The interpretation we make of these facts is that females 15–29 have consistently been enumerated almost fully (98.6 per cent complete), and that the deficiencies in births estimated from females 30 and over, under 15, and from males 5–59, are the result of greater net undercounts among these groups. The consequent implication that in some censuses females 55–64 were undercounted as much as 18 to 21 per cent is somewhat startling.

Not all of this net undercount need be the result of omission from the census of females whose true age is 55–64. Some of the undercount can be the result of net losses from this age-group through erroneous age reporting. We have considered, in fact, the hypothesis that *all* of the undercounting of women 30 and over is the result of age misstatement. The implications of this hypothesis will now be explored.

(*a*) If the undercount of females 30 and over resulted wholly from age misreporting, females under 30 would necessarily be *overcounted*. Presumably the overcounting would concentrate in the age range 15–29. This overcounting would have been greatest in the early censuses (when the undercounts at the ages above 30 were the greatest). In other words, the true size of the cohorts 15–29 in the early censuses would be *less* than the enumerated females—substantially less if the large undercounts at ages over 30 in these censuses are to be explained in this way.

(b) If we knew that females 15–29 were actually fewer than reported, we would necessarily estimate smaller expected cohorts of children at the earlier censuses. That is, if the number of 15 to 29-year-old females in each census were inflated by an amount equal to the estimated undercount at ages 30 and over in that census, allowance for this inflation would substantially reduce the number of children estimated by the backward projection of these females. The result of estimating substantially smaller birth cohorts would in fact be estimated *overcounts* of children 0–4. In constructing Table 5, the missing women at ages 30 and over were assumed to have been recorded in the age group 15–29. The table shows the effect of allowing for this age misstatement on the number of children projected backward from these females.

TABLE 5

Per Cent Undercount[a] Implied for Native White Females 0–4 by Assumption that Women Omitted over 30 Were Reported as 15–29

			Per Cent Undercount of Females 0–4	
Year	Implied Per Cent Undercount for Females 20–24	Year	Implied by Assumption Omitted Females Over 30 Were Reported as 15–29	Implied by Assumption Females 15–29 Were Undercounted in Each Census by 1.4 Per Cent
1880	−15.9	1860	−5.8	10.1
1890	−17.2	1870	—	—
1900	−16.0	1880	−6.9	9.1
1910	−14.5	1890	−9.5	5.0
1920	−14.1	1900	−7.6	6.5
1930	−14.9	1910	−7.5	7.4
1940	− 7.7	1920	−1.1	6.6
1950	− 4.2	1930	2.4	6.6

[a] Minus entry indicates an overcount.

On this basis, the number of children 0–4 in the censuses from 1860 to 1920 (excluding 1870 since no estimate was prepared for this census) appear to be overcounted.[8] This implication of age misstatement rather than net omission among older

[8] In 1930 the undercount originally estimated is reduced, but does not become an overcount.

59

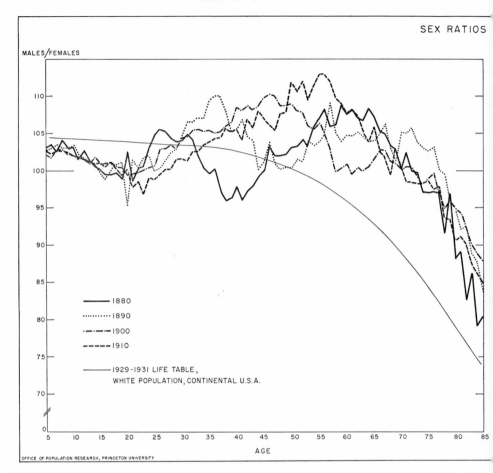

FIGURE 17*a*.   Sex Ratios of Age Heaping Adjusted Populations, Ages
5–85, 1880–1910, and Sex Ratios Based on 1929–1931 Life Tables.

women appears highly implausible, and is in fact not in accord
with other evidence concerning the errors occurring in the enumeration of children. In contrast, our assumption of near completeness of enumeration of the females 15–29 years old gives a
plausible sequence of net undercounts of children in the several
censuses (see Figure 15).

(*c*) Similarly, the hypothesis that the apparent omissions at
ages 30 and over were really the result of age misstatement con-
tradicts the evidence cited in Chapter 2 indicating that females
15–29 have actually been slightly undercounted in recent
censuses.

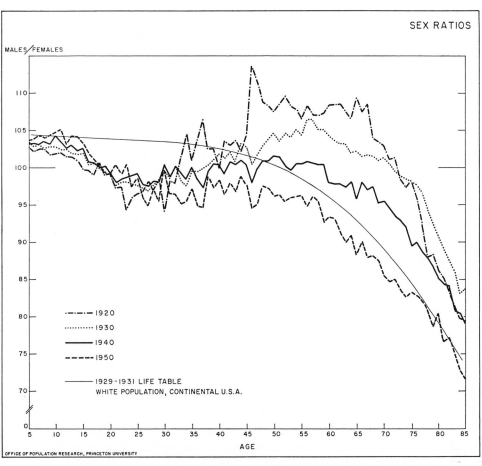

FIGURE 17*b*. Sex Ratios of Age Heaping Adjusted Populations, Ages 5–85, 1920–1950, and Sex Ratios Based on 1929–1931 Life Tables.

(*d*) In addition, if this hypothesis were true, and our birth estimates were made consistent with a much smaller number of females 15–29, the result would be estimated overcounts for males at almost all ages in all censuses. The reasoning underlying this argument is similar to the argument presented in (*b*) above and is a result of the fact that the estimates for the two sexes are not independent, but are tied together by the sex ratio at birth.

(*e*) Finally, if the hypothesis were true, the overcounts 15–29 among females in early censuses would have produced a low masculinity ratio in this age span, which would have tended toward a normal ratio (slightly above unity at these ages) as undercounts among females over 30 diminished. As Figure 17 shows, no such trend in sex ratios exists over this age span.

THE EFFECT OF ADJUSTED SURVIVORSHIP RATES ON ESTIMATED UNDERCOUNTS

We have estimated births and census enumeration errors using estimates of mortality which (we have suggested) are themselves in error because of the incorrect population size used as the denominator in their calculation. How have our estimates of births and expected populations been affected by errors in estimated mortality? Or, to phrase the question differently, if we had had available our adjusted mortality estimates before estimating births and enumeration errors, how different would these estimates have been? We will provide an answer about enumeration errors in the form of alternative estimates based on the adjusted estimates of mortality. Alternative estimates for births have not been calculated because the effect here, as we will try to demonstrate, is negligible. However, the two sets of estimates are so intimately related, and the logical argument is so well confirmed by the evidence (i.e., our alternative estimates of enumeration errors), that we will first present this argument and then the confirmation.

For purposes of exposition, let us assume that our estimates of births are based solely on females 15–29, and that we are concerned only with errors in the enumeration of females. Mortality rates under 15 would then be overstated because of undercounts among females at these ages, and the estimated number of births would be slightly too large.[9] The overstatement of the number of births results from allowing for too many deaths at ages 5–14 in projecting backward; this overstatement of mortality is in turn a consequence of the under-enumeration at these ages.[10] We have not calculated the exact effect of this source of error on our birth estimates, but it is clearly not very large.[11]

Thus the effect of overestimated mortality is consequential

[9] These effects would occur only in mortality rates after 1900, because estimates for the nineteenth century are drawn from model life tables, not directly dependent on United States data.

[10] The official U.S. life tables we have used were adjusted, in their construction, for under-enumeration of children 0–4.

[11] Survivorship rates at these ages (5–14) are extremely high; any increase resulting from an adjustment of mortality for under-enumeration will be insignificant.

only for estimated errors in enumeration over age 30, at least in the female population. We have constructed expected populations among females over 30 that were too small, because we have used excessively high death rates. In other words, given our birth estimates, lower estimates of mortality would generate larger expected populations and larger estimates of census enumeration errors. The effect becomes quite large at upper ages because: (a) the undercounts are large, and (b) mortality rates are high so that a given per cent adjustment in mortality has a large effect on survivorship. A 10 per cent increase in a mortality rate of 10 per cent has as great an effect on survivorship as doubling a 1 per cent mortality rate. The adjustments in mortality and consequently in the estimates of under-enumeration should have the greatest effect the earlier the census (in the twentieth century) because of the higher rates of under-enumeration and the lower rates of survival, and the greater the age because of the cumulative effect of the overstatement of mortality.

In effect then, the large undercounts we have estimated for females at ages 30 and over are not maximum estimates. In fact, the likelihood is that our estimates of under-enumeration at these ages are too low and that a more accurate measure is provided by our alternative estimates of under-enumeration.

Before presenting these alternative estimates, we will indicate the effect the incorrect (i.e., overstated) mortality estimates have had on our projections of males, both backward and forward. It should be recalled that the birth estimates derived from males aged 5–59 were increased to a level consistent with the birth estimates derived from females 15–29. If we had used lower estimates of mortality (resulting from adjustments to the life tables for under-enumeration) in estimating births from males 5–59, the most significant effect would have been to *increase* the per cent difference between births estimated from males and births estimated from females. Reduced estimates of mortality would have generated fewer births. Instead of an over-all difference of 3 per cent between the births estimated from the two sexes, the difference would have been $(3 + x)$ per cent.

At the same time, however, the adjusted estimates of (male) mortality would have had some small effect on the yearly fluctuations of births because of the differential changes in the adjusted life tables. This effect is also minimal because of the

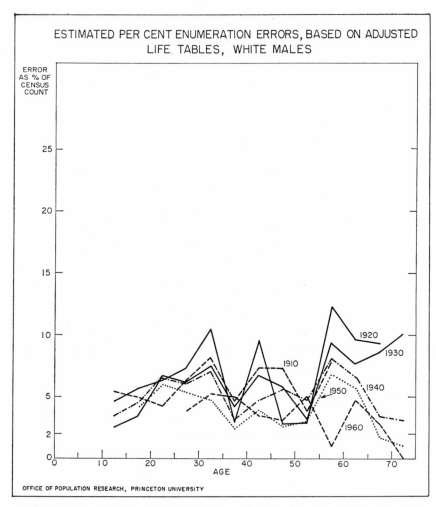

FIGURE 18. Estimated Per Cent Census Enumeration Errors Based on Life Tables Adjusted for Under-Enumeration, Native White Males, 1910–1950 and Total White Males, 1960.
Source: Table 21

averaging technique we have used in preparing the final series of estimated births.

In regard to the estimation of expected populations, the use of overestimates of mortality has the same general effect on males as on females—expected populations which are too small, and increasingly so with age. The difference between the two sets of

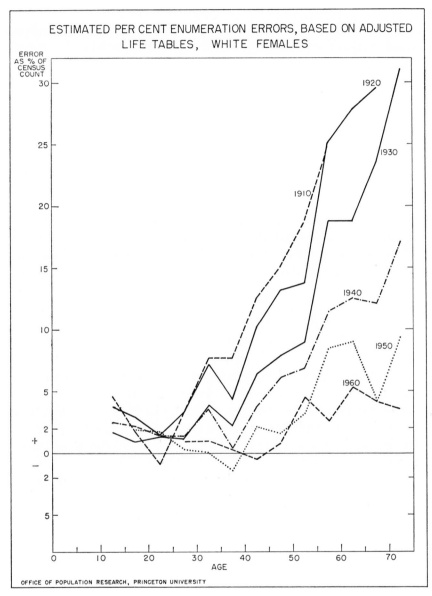

FIGURE 19.   Estimated Per Cent Census Enumeration Errors Based on Life
Tables Adjusted for Under-Enumeration, Native White Females, 1910–1950 and
Total White Females, 1960.
Source: Table 22

expected populations is not as great with the males as with the females (resulting from the smaller original estimates of under-enumeration for the males). The use of the adjusted estimates of male mortality has the effect, however, of eliminating, for 70–74 in 1940, 65–74 in 1950, and 70–74 in 1960, the overcounts originally estimated for males.[12]

The alternative estimates of under-enumeration are shown in Figures 18 and 19. A comparison of these errors with our original estimates (see Figures 13 and 14) reveals very little difference at the younger ages; as expected, the differences become increasingly pronounced with age. A few points are worthy of comment:

1. As we have previously noted, the use of adjusted mortality completely eliminated the overcounts originally estimated for males, up to ages 70–74, in the 1940, 1950, and 1960 censuses.

2. The alternative male estimates show a general improvement from one census to the next, excluding 1960, for the age groups 55–59 and over. This progression was not as consistent in the original set of estimates.

3. The 1960 male estimates are relatively level instead of dropping off sharply with age.

4. As to adjusted female undercounts, the point most worthy of comment is the increasing level of error with age[13] (aside from instances already described, e.g., 65–69 in 1940 and 1950, and 55–59 in 1960) and the consistent improvement from one census to the next. In contrast, the original estimates did not always show increases with age.

We have not used these alternative estimates of under-enumeration to adjust the total white populations or to revise our birth rate estimates. However, the patterns shown in Figures 18 and 19 lead us to believe that these alternative estimates may be closer to the truth than the original estimates.

---

[12] It was not possible to extend our alternative estimates beyond 70–74 for males in 1950 and 1960. For the problem involved, and the specific methods used to prepare the alternative estimates, see Chapter 9.

Even if it had been possible to continue our alternative estimates to higher ages, it is unlikely that we would have eliminated all of the overcounts at the extreme older ages, since some of the overcounting is doubtless real, a result of age misstatement.

[13] Up to ages 55–58 in 1910, 65–68 in 1920, and 70–74 in 1930, 1940, 1950, and 1960.

Part III
TECHNIQUES OF ANALYSIS AND ESTIMATION

Chapter 6. The Relation between Total Fertility and the Birth Rate

Standard summary measures of fertility—e.g., the general fertility rate, the total fertility rate, and the gross reproduction rate—have been devised to minimize or remove the influence of intervening elements such as the age composition that can play an important part in determining the crude birth rate. This chapter explains what factors cause a variable relation between a "pure" measure of fertility—the total fertility rate—and the crude birth rate. The explanation does not cover all possible demographic circumstances, but it does cover a wide range, including those experienced in the United States since 1800. It provides the needed technical support for statements made in Chapter 4.

Fertility Measures Defined

The annual *crude birth rate* is defined as the number of births during a year divided by the average size of the population during the year. It measures the fertility of the population as a whole, rather than of that segment of the population biologically capable of bearing children.

The *general fertility rate* is defined as births divided by the average number of women of childbearing age. This rate is obviously unaffected by the proportion of the population who are women of childbearing age, but it is influenced by variations in the age distribution *within* the childbearing span.

Childbearing performance within this span is described by the age-schedule of fertility—the proportion of women at each age producing a live birth. The area under this schedule—the *total fertility rate*—is a useful summary measure of female childbearing performance. If the fertility schedule records the childbearing history of a group of women born in the same year (a birth cohort) as they move through life, the total fertility rate is the average number of children born at the completion of childbearing. If (as is more frequently the case) the schedule expresses the fertility of a cross-section of the population during a particular period, total fertility can be viewed as the average number of births that would occur to a hypothetical cohort of women subject through its life to the given fertility schedule.

The *gross reproduction rate* is identical to total fertility except that it sums female births only, so that it indicates the total number of *daughters* that would be born.

RELATIONS AMONG FERTILITY MEASURES

Two factors determine the relationship between the birth rate and the total fertility rate: first, the age and sex distribution of the population, and second, the shape of the fertility schedule. Since childbearing is restricted to women in the general age range of 15 to 44, the most significant feature of the age-sex distribution is the proportion of the total population who are women 15–44. A less important element, but still sometimes a consequential one, is the age distribution *within* the childbearing span, and its relation to the shape of the fertility function. Human age-specific schedules usually rise smoothly from low values at the earliest childbearing age to a single peak in the range of 23–30 years and then decline smoothly toward zero at the latest childbearing ages.

A population with a given proportion 15–44 and a given fertility schedule has a relatively high birth rate if the ages at which the greatest numbers occur *within* this span are also the ages with the peak rates of childbearing. Specifically, the highest possible birth rate from a given fertility schedule and a given proportion 15–44 would result if *all* of the women within this span were at the age of highest fertility. More generally, the birth rate is elevated by a positive linear correlation between the numbers at each age within the childbearing span and the fertility at each age.

If F is total fertility, B the crude birth rate, $c(a)da$ the proportion of the population consisting of women in the age interval a to $a + da$, α and β are the lower and upper limits of childbearing, and $f(a)da$ is the proportion of women a to $a + da$ bearing a child, then

(1) $$F = \int_\alpha^\beta f(a)da$$

and

(2) $$B = \int_\alpha^\beta c(a)f(a)da$$

The correlation between $c(a)$ and $f(a)$ over the childbearing interval is:

$$(3) \qquad r_{fc} = \frac{\int_\alpha^\beta f(a)c(a)da - \dfrac{\int_\alpha^\beta f(a)da \int_\alpha^\beta c(a)da}{\beta - \alpha}}{\sigma_f \cdot \sigma_c(\beta - \alpha)}$$

where σ_f and σ_c are the standard deviation of fertility and the proportionate age distribution in the interval α to β (note that $f(a)$ and $c(a)$ are *not* frequency distributions, but two variables being correlated. The relevant frequency distribution is a uniform density of points over the interval).

It follows that:

$$(4) \qquad B = r_{fc}\sigma_f\sigma_c(\beta - \alpha) + \frac{F}{\beta - \alpha}\int_\alpha^\beta c(a)da$$

If the correlation is zero, the birth rate equals average annual fertility over the childbearing span $\left(\text{i.e., } \dfrac{F}{\beta - \alpha}\right)$ times the proportion of the population who are women of childbearing age. If the correlation is positive, the birth rate exceeds this value, if negative, it falls short.

The relationship expressed in (4) can be broken into two relationships among the three most common summary measures of fertility. The third common measure is the *general fertility rate* (G) defined as births per woman 15–44. The final pair of relations is then:

$$(5) \qquad B = G\int_\alpha^\beta c(a)da$$

$$(6) \qquad G = \frac{F}{\beta - \alpha} + r_{fc}\sigma_f\sigma_c \frac{\beta - \alpha}{\int_\alpha^\beta c(a)da}$$

General fertility equals total fertility divided by the number of years in the childbearing span plus a term expressing the effect of interaction (if any) between the form of the age distribution within the span and the fertility schedule. It should be noted for completeness that the Gross Reproduction Rate is simply total fertility multiplied by the proportion of total births that are female.

The birth rate is depressed by a negative correlation. The effect of correlation between fertility and the age distribution within the childbearing span is illustrated by United States

71

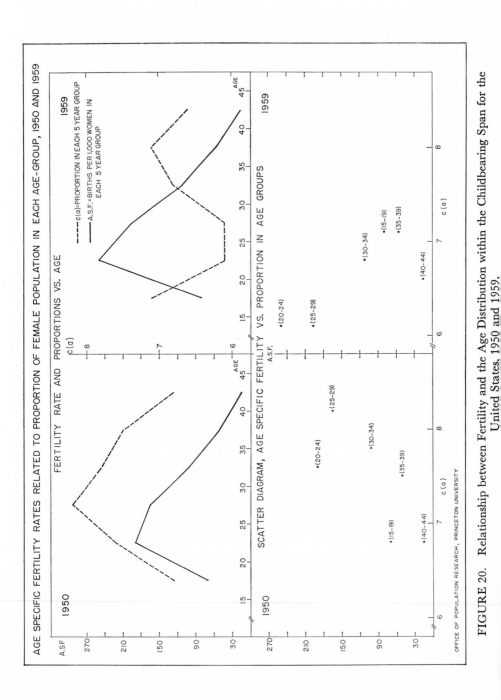

FIGURE 20. Relationship between Fertility and the Age Distribution within the Childbearing Span for the United States, 1950 and 1959.

experience in the 1950's. As Figure 20 shows, there was a positive correlation in 1950, and a negative correlation in 1959. As a result, a 19.1 per cent increase in total white fertility was accompanied by only a 12.0 per cent increase in general fertility (births per woman 15–44), and a 1.2 per cent rise in the birth rate. The fact that the smallest age group (20–24) in 1959 occurred at the maximum fertility rate offset some of the rise in total fertility. A further—and larger—offset resulted from the decline in the proportion 15–44 so that the birth rate hardly increased at all.

When fertility has been constant, or has been steadily declining, a conspicuous "hollow" such as that centered on age 25 in the 1959 age distribution does not occur. With a history of constant or continuously declining fertility, the age distribution assumes a roughly linear form in the range 15–44. Under these circumstances the correlation between fertility and the age distribution is about zero when the fertility schedule is symmetrical, and when the mean age of childbearing coincides with the midpoint (age 30) of the interval 15–44. If (as was the case in the United States until the 1950's) the roughly linear age distribution declines as age increases, a positive correlation between fertility and age distribution within the span 15–44 arises when the mean age of childbearing is below 30 years, and a negative correlation when the mean age is over 30. Positive correlation results from a low mean age because the high fertility levels near the mean age occur at the young ages when there are more than average numbers, and low fertility (at ages distant from the mean) occur at older ages when numbers are relatively small. Thus with an age distribution that falls steadily through the childbearing span, a given total fertility rate produces a higher birth rate when childbearing occurs early, and lower when it occurs late.[1]

Trends in Total Fertility Versus Trends in the Birth Rate in the United States, 1800–1960

Estimates of total fertility in the United States, 1800–1960, are shown in Table 2 and Figure 10, Chapter 4. In Figure 11

[1] Ansley J. Coale, and C. Y. Tye, "The Significance of Age-Patterns of Fertility in High Fertility Populations," Milbank Memorial Fund *Quarterly*, Vol. XXXIX, No. 4 (October 1961), pp. 631–646.

in Chapter 4, birth rates and the total fertility rate are shown as index numbers, with the value for 1890 as 100. Note that until 1948, the two indexes are closely parallel. In view of the effect of the age distribution and the shape of the fertility schedule on the birth rate with given total fertility, this parallelism can only be regarded as anomalous, especially since the age distribution and the mean age of childbearing have been subject to major changes. The next two sections of this chapter are devoted to explaining this anomaly. The explanation is necessarily quite technical. Before becoming involved in technical details, we will outline the essential points of the argument.

The age distribution of any population is determined dominantly by its fertility history, unless it has been subject to heavy age-selective migration, or to very extensive age-selective military casualties. The age distribution can often be understood by considering first the *stable* age distribution associated with current levels of fertility, and second, the modifications in that stable distribution implicit in the actual fertility history.

A stable age distribution with moderate fertility (a total fertility of 3.5 to 4.0 births, as in the United States at about the turn of the century) has the maximum proportion aged 15–44. At higher fertility levels, the population has a preponderance under 15 at the expense of the 15–44 group, and at lower levels of fertility, the relatively large proportion over 45 diminishes the proportion in the childbearing span. The proportion 15–44 in the stable population consistent with 1890 fertility and mortality was about 1.08 times the proportion consistent with the much higher fertility of 1800, and about 1.10 times the proportion consistent with the much lower fertility of the 1930's. Thus the decline in fertility from 1800 to 1934 would in itself have led to a rise in the birth rate relative to total fertility of about 8 per cent, followed by a decline of about 10 per cent.

The major source of variation at each point in time from the stable age distribution was the fact that fertility had been declining rather than remaining constant. As will be shown later in this chapter, a history of constantly falling birth rates produces a larger fraction aged 15–44 than is found in the current stable population. This effect is the greater (a) the greater has been the recent annual per cent rate of decrease in fertility, and (b) the lower is the current fertility rate. The past history of declining fertility increased the proportion 15–44 above that found in the stable population by a negligible extent

$$\left(\frac{\text{proportion 15–44 with declining fertility}}{\text{proportion 15–44 in stable population}} < 1.01\right)$$

before 1830. By 1890 the ratio had reached 1.06, and by 1935 1.16, as a result of the very low current fertility and a recent history of rapid decline. Thus in the nineteenth century the increase in the proportion 15–44 in the stable age distribution was *accentuated* by an increasing effect of the past history of declining fertility from higher levels; and from 1900–1935, a declining proportion 15–44 in the stable population was *countered* by further increases of the positive effect of formerly higher fertility rates.

A third element that affected the relation between the birth rate and the total fertility rate was the changing shape of the fertility schedule, and its changing correlation with the age distribution within the childbearing span. The average age of childbearing in the United States has always been low relative to most European countries, because of a persistent tendency toward younger marriage in America than in Europe. Young childbearing causes a positive correlation between the age distribution and the fertility schedule when the age distribution slopes downward from age 15 to 45. A steep downward slope is caused by high fertility (in this instance high fertility 15 to 45 years in the past). Such a combination of high fertility and early childbearing is especially conducive to a birth rate that is high relative to expectations based on the total fertility rate and the proportion of women 15–44.[2]

Early childbearing in the United States had a steadily diminishing effect from 1800 until 1940 in promoting a high birth rate relative to total fertility. The effect diminished during the nine-

[2] Consider an equation given earlier (Equation 4) p. 71,

$$B = r_{fc}\sigma_f\sigma_c(\beta - \alpha) + \frac{F}{\beta - \alpha}\int_{\alpha}^{\beta} c(a)\,da$$

Early childbearing and a downsloping age distribution assure a positive value of r_{fc}. A steeply downsloping age distribution leads to a large value of σ_c and yields an especially high birth rate relative to fertility and the proportion in the childbearing ages.

teenth century because of lessening steepness of the age distribution and rising age at marriage.[3] In 1830, early childbearing had the effect of multiplying the birth rate (the birth rate the same total fertility centered on age thirty would have produced) by about 1.10. By 1900 the augmenting effect of young childbearing had diminished to about 1.03.

It was noted earlier that during the nineteenth century the proportion in the childbearing ages in the stable population was increasing; an increase reinforced in the actual age distribution by the rising inflationary effect of a past history of declining fertility. We now note that these tendencies, which operated to increase the birth rate relative to the total fertility rate, were offset by a major decline in the importance of early childbearing as a source of a higher birth rate.[4]

From about 1890 until the 1930's, the effect of early childbearing on the relation of the birth rate to total fertility was of minor importance because (a) age at marriage and mean age of childbearing changed only slightly, and (b) the age distribution in the childbearing ages during this period was at no time very steep, as it had been earlier. However, between 1890 and the mid 1930's, the stable age distribution became much less favorable to the birth rate—a development just about exactly offset by the increasingly *favorable* effect of the past history of declining fertility. From 1935 to 1957 total fertility rose. This development produced a stable age distribution more favorable to the birth rate. On the other hand, a history of rising fertility reduces the proportion in the childbearing ages relative to the stable population. The combination (after 1935) of a recent history of rising fertility and a more remote history of falling fertility has an

[3] An increase in average age at marriage in the 19th century can be inferred from scattered state records, and less reliably from informal impressions of observers. Thomas P. Monohan, *The Pattern of Age at Marriage in the United States*, Vol. I, Philadelphia: Privately printed, 1951; and an observation by Benjamin Franklin in 1751, cited in W. H. Grabill, C. V. Kiser, and P. K. Whelpton, *The Fertility of American Women* (New York: John Wiley, 1958), pp. 5–6.

[4] It must be recognized that we are here considering a relation between two measures (the birth rate and the total fertility rate) both of which are *period* or *cross-sectional* measures of fertility. We are not attempting (because the basic data do not provide the means) to make estimates of *cohort* fertility. We call attention to this point because the changing age-pattern of marriage and childbearing that characterized the nineteenth century and the 1940's and 1950's was the *source* of important changes in period fertility, and was attended by changing relations between period and cohort fertility.

effect on the age distribution too complex for analysis here. The actual outcome of these trends has been a recent birth rate that is *low* given the total fertility rate. In fact for the first time in the history of the Republic, in 1954 the actual birth rate fell below the intrinsic birth rate (the birth rate in the corresponding stable population).

The anomalous results that we set out to explain on page 74 (the fact that from 1830 to the 1940's the birth rate and the total fertility rate changed in about the same proportion) turn out to be the fortuitous outcome of offsetting factors. The two rates *could* have behaved divergently if during the nineteenth century the effect of an increasing proportion aged 15–44 arising from a changing stable age distribution reinforced by the effect of the decline in fertility had not been offset by the decreasing importance of early childbearing. They might have diverged from 1890 to 1940 if the unfavorable changes in the stable age distribution had not been offset by the increasingly favorable effect on the actual distribution of the past history of declining fertility. The fortuitous nature of the parallel course of the two measures is graphically demonstrated by their markedly divergent movement in the 1950's.[5] In 1957 the birth rate was equal to the birth rate in 1924, although total fertility was 20.4 per cent higher. In fact, total fertility in 1957 is the highest in the century.

In the next two sections, the determination of the proportion aged 15–44 in the stable population, and the effect of declining fertility on the age distribution will be discussed in greater detail. Our discussion has asserted certain relationships and explored their implications for the birth rate. In these sections the basis of these assertions will be explained.

THE PROPORTION AGED 15–44 IN STABLE
    AGE DISTRIBUTIONS

The principal determinant of the gross form of a stable age distribution is fertility—primarily the level of fertility, as expressed by the total fertility rate, although the mean age of the fertility schedule is also sometimes influential.[6] However,

[5] See p. 73 above.

[6] Louis I. Dublin, and Alfred J. Lotka, "On the True Rate of Natural Increase," *Journal of the American Statistical Association*, September, 1925, 151, pp. 305–339; J. Bourgeois-Pichat, "Utilisation de la notion de population stable pour mesurer

PART III. CHAPTER 6

variations in the proportion aged 15–44 in the stable age distributions are relatively minor in response to differences in fertility. Moreover, differences in the level of mortality, which have only a slight effect on the over-all form of the age distribution, have a tangible influence on the proportions aged 15–44.

The reason that fertility differences (within the range of commonly observed levels of fertility) have little effect on the proportion aged 15–44 is that (as Lotka showed in 1925) a slightly higher fertility produces a stable age distribution that differs from a lower fertility distribution as the result of a kind of "pivoting" action on the mean age of the distribution. The higher fertility population has higher proportions at all ages below the mean, and lower proportions at all ages above the mean.

The mean age of the stable population (when total fertility is within the range of 2 to 8 births per woman) always falls within the childbearing span. Hence the "pivoting" that expresses the difference in age distribution resulting from a difference in fertility always involves an increase in some age-groups within the childbearing span, and a decrease in others. When the age of pivoting is below 30, the population with the lower fertility has fewer women in the small segment of the childbearing span below the pivot, and more women in the larger segment above the pivot. Hence when fertility is very high, a slightly lower fertility is associated with a larger fraction in the childbearing ages. A similar argument shows that when fertility is very low, a lower fertility stable population has a smaller fraction in the childbearing ages. Figure 21 shows the association between the proportion 15–44 and total fertility, at a given level of mortality (i.e., with a fixed life table).

Differences in mortality affect the proportion aged 15–44 in stable populations because the typical effect of lower mortality is to raise the proportion under 15, and often to increase the

la mortalité et la fécondité des populations des pays sous-developpés." *Bulletin de l'Institut International de Statistique*, Tome 36, 2° Livraison, pp. 94–121, Stockholm, 1958; Ansley J. Coale, "The Effects of Changes in Mortality and Fertility on Age Composition," Milbank Memorial Fund *Quarterly*, Vol. XXXIV, No. 1 (January 1956), pp. 79–114; Ansley J. Coale, "How the Age Distribution of a Human Population is Determined," *Cold Spring Harbour Symposia on Quantitative Biology*, Vol. XXII (1957); Coale and Tye, *op. cit.*

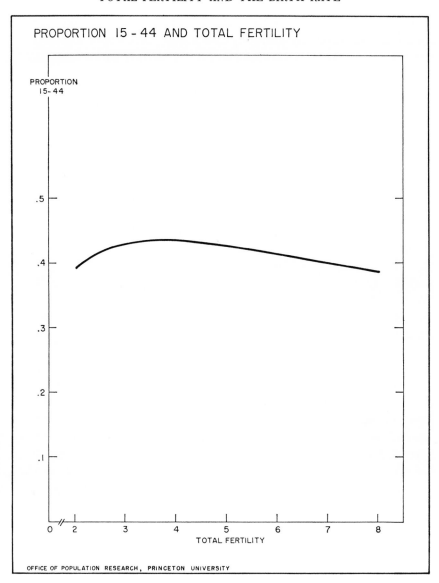

FIGURE 21.   Relation between Proportion of Women 15–44
and Total Fertility, Mortality Held Constant.

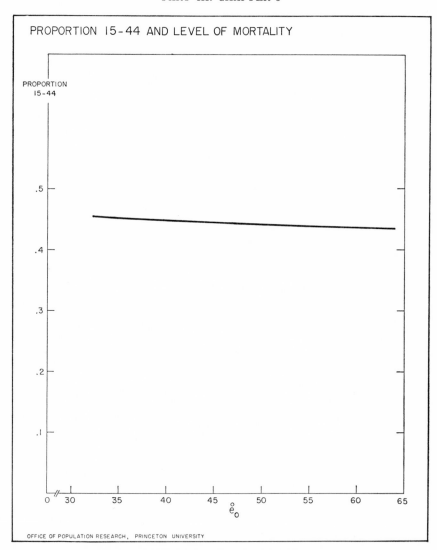

FIGURE 22.   Relation between Proportion of Women 15–44
and Level of Mortality, Fertility Held Constant.

proportion at the older ages as well.[7] While the general pattern
of a steeply declining distribution associated with high fertility,

[7] Ansley J. Coale, "The Effect of Declines in Mortality on Age Distribution,"
Trends and Differentials in Mortality, Milbank Memorial Fund, New York, 1956,
pp. 125–132; Ansley J. Coale, "How the Age Distribution of a Human Population
is Determined," *Cold Spring Harbor Symposia on Quantitative Biology,* Vol. XXII,
1957.

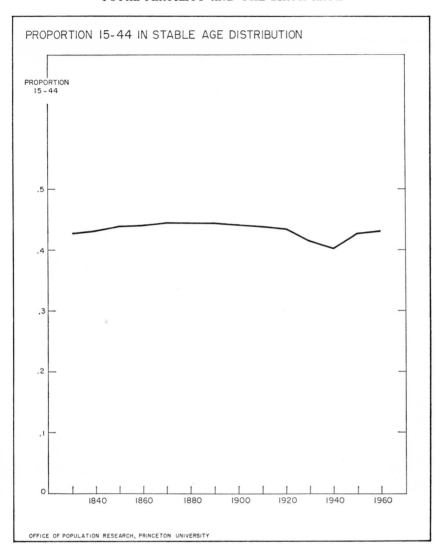

PROPORTION 15-44 IN STABLE AGE DISTRIBUTION

OFFICE OF POPULATION RESEARCH, PRINCETON UNIVERSITY

FIGURE 23.   Proportion 15–44 in United States White
Female Stable Age Distributions, 1830–1960.

and a relatively "flat" distribution with low fertility is not
affected by differences in mortality, the level of mortality does
influence the proportion 15–44. This effect is shown in Figure 22,
where the proportion 15–44 at various levels of mortality (characterized by expectation of life at birth) are indicated with a

constant moderate level of fertility (total fertility rate about four children).

In the United States, estimated total fertility of white women fell from about 7.0 in 1800 to about 2.2 in the 1930's. At the same time expectation of life at birth rose from a value probably somewhat below 40 years to 67 years in 1940, and over 73 years in 1960. Estimated proportions 15–44 in the corresponding stable age distributions (as both fertility and mortality changed) are shown in Figure 23.

The Effect of Declining Fertility on the Age Distribution

Suppose that there are two female populations with the following characteristics:

a) Both have the same fertility and the same number of births at a given moment ($t = 0$).

b) Both have shared the same history of *mortality risks* at each age. Moreover, the risks prevailing at the given moment have prevailed in the past.

c) One female population has experienced the now prevalent fertility without change in the past, the other has experienced fertility that, at every age, has been changing by a fixed proportion each year. For the second population the general fertility rate has followed a course:

$$(7) \qquad\qquad f(t) = f(0)e^{kt}$$

The question at issue is a comparison of the *age distributions* that would result from these two sets of circumstances. The age distribution resulting from constant fertility and mortality is Lotka's stable age distribution given by the equation:

$$(8) \qquad\qquad c(a) = be^{-ra}p(a)$$

where $c(a)$ is the proportion at age a, b is the birth rate, r is the constant (intrinsic) rate of increase, and $p(a)$ is the proportion surviving from birth to age a.

Associated with this stable age distribution are annual births growing at a constant annual rate of increase (r). If time is measured from the moment ($t = 0$) where the two populations have the same number of births, the birth sequence in the stable population is given by:

(9) $$B_s(t) = B(0)e^{rt}$$

The birth sequence associated with *declining* fertility must satisfy the following integral equation:

(10) $$B(t) = \int_0^\omega B(t - a)p(a)m(a,t)da$$

or

(10a) $$B(t) = \int_0^\omega B(t - a)p(a)m(a)e^{kt}da$$

where $m(a,t)$ is the age-specific fertility rate (of female births) at time t, $m(a)$ is the rate at $t = 0$, and $p(a)$ is the proportion of females surviving from birth to age a. An approximate solution to Eq. (10a) can be obtained by assuming, for analytical simplicity, that all births occur at the mean age of childbearing, A. Eq. (10a) then becomes:

(11) $$B(t) = B(t - a)p(A)m(A)e^{kt}$$

$p(A)m(A)$ is seen to be the Net Reproduction Rate at $t = 0$. Hence $p(A)m(A)$ equals e^{rA} where r is the intrinsic rate of increase at $t = 0$. Thus Eq. (11) can be written as:

(12) $$B(t) = B(t - A)e^{rA+kt}$$

Let $y(t) = \log_e B(t)$, then

(13) $$y(t) - y(t - A) = rA + kt$$

This is a first-order non-homogeneous difference equation. Its solution leads to the following expression for births:

(14) $$B(t) = B(0)e^{\left(r + \frac{k}{2}\right)t + \frac{k}{2A}t^2}$$

This expression is analogous to the stable population first-order exponential Eq. (3); in fact Eq. (8) reduces to Eq. (3) if $k = 0$.

It should be noted that the sequence of births specified in Eq. (14) is only an approximate solution of Equations (10) and (10a) because it is derived on the assumption that all births occur at age A. Strictly speaking, the solution to the difference equation defines a sequence of births occurring at discrete points in time, points separated by intervals of A years. However, every point on the continuous function defined by Eq. (14) satisfies the difference equation; and if an initial age distribution were consistent with Eq. (14), the ensuing births would all conform to Eq. (14).

The usefulness of Eq. (14) depends on how closely the birth sequence it describes satisfies the integral Eq. (10), where no assumption is made that all births occur at age A, and on whether the birth sequence tends to converge on Eq. (14) from arbitrary initial conditions. With the age-schedules of fertility actually observed in human populations, the substitution of Eq. (14) in Eq. (10) produces an integral that differs from the prescribed value by at most a few per cent. Also, if Eq. (14) were an exact expression of the birth sequence starting from the appropriate age distribution, then, as proved by Alvaro Lopez,[8] the actual sequence would converge from arbitrary initial conditions to this sequence.

To show the effect of a past history of constantly changing fertility on the age distribution, we now compare the birth sequence defined by Eq. (14) with the birth sequence that would have resulted from a past history of fertility constant at the schedule prevailing at the given moment, Eq. (9). If Eq. (14) is divided by Eq. (9) for values of t preceding $t = 0$, we find:

$$(15) \qquad \frac{B_d(-t)}{B_s(-t)} = e^{\frac{k}{2}(-t) + \frac{k}{2A}(-t)^2}$$

where $B_d(-t)$ represents the births with a history of declining fertility, and $B_s(-t)$ the births in the stable population.

Figure 24 shows Eq. (15) plotted for various rates of decline in fertility. Note that the population with a history of declining fertility has slightly more births in the A years preceding $t = 0$, the same number at $t = -A$, and rapidly diminishing numbers at times more than A years before. Eq. (15) has immediate relevance for the age distribution resulting from a history of declining fertility. It shows the numbers at each age relative to the number in the stable age distribution with the same mortality, and the fertility of the given moment. To find the declining-

---

[8] Alvaro Lopez, *Problems in Stable Age Distribution Theory* (Princeton: Office of Population Research, Princeton University, 1961).

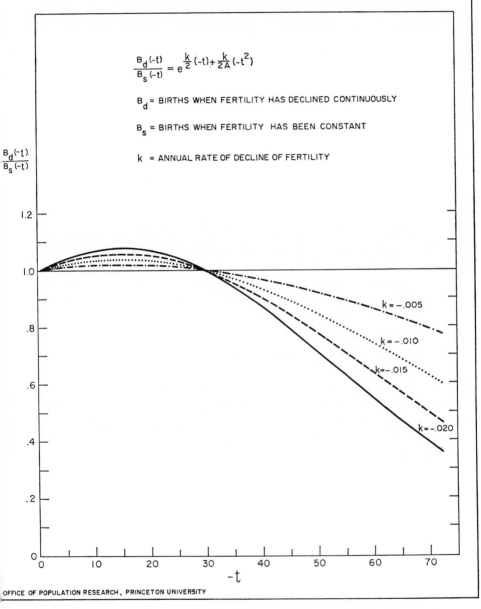

FIGURE 24.   Birth Sequence in a Population with Constant Fertility Compared to Birth Sequence in a Population with Declining Fertility, for Various Rates of Decline in Fertility.

fertility proportionate age distribution, one multiplies the number at each age in the stable age distribution by $e^{-\frac{k}{2}a + \frac{k}{2A}a^2}$. Since this function is only slightly above one in the age range 0 to A, and falls relatively far below one at older ages, the total number in the declining fertility distribution will fall below the number in the stable distribution. Therefore the *proportions* at age 0 and age A (where by assumption the *numbers* are equal) are greater in the declining-fertility population.

It is the small number of births found more than 40 or 50 years ago in the population with a history of fertility that has declined from higher levels that accounts for the higher proportion it has in the childbearing ages, and for its higher birth rate, relative to the stable population. It may seem anomalous that a population with a history of declining fertility should have a history of fewer births (more than A years ago) than a population with a history of constant fertility. The following qualitative argument may help clarify this peculiar result. A history of declining fertility has two opposing implications for the preceding birth sequence: on the one hand the higher fertility of the past tends to produce more births; on the other hand the higher past fertility implies faster prior growth, a smaller earlier population, and hence a tendency to produce a smaller number of births in the past. The effect of higher fertility predominates in the immediate past, while the effect of more rapid growth, which is *compounded* in the more remote past, predominates at times more than A years before $t = 0$. The number of births at some time about A years before $t = 0$ must be equal for any pair of contrasting fertility histories, if it is assumed that the sequences being compared are characterized by the same number of births and the same fertility at $t = 0$. For if births and fertility are equal, the number of mothers must be about the same, and hence there must have been the same number of births in the two sequences about A years before.

The fact that $e^{-\frac{k}{2}a + \frac{k}{2A}a^2}$ is much less than one for ages past 45, and only slightly over one at ages under 30 is responsible for the fact that the population with a history of declining fertility has a higher proportion of women in the childbearing ages. This effect may be visualized by representing the declining-fertility

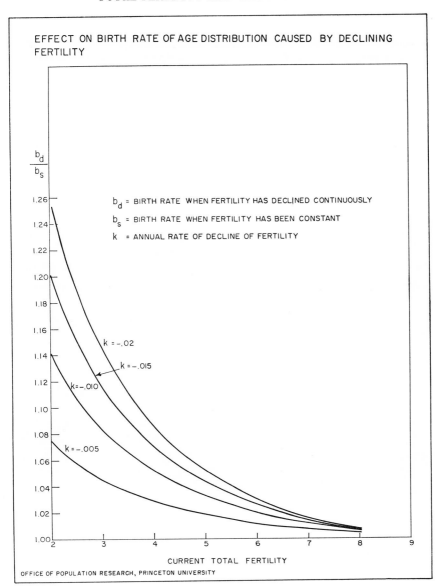

EFFECT ON BIRTH RATE OF AGE DISTRIBUTION CAUSED BY DECLINING FERTILITY

b_d = BIRTH RATE WHEN FERTILITY HAS DECLINED CONTINUOUSLY

b_s = BIRTH RATE WHEN FERTILITY HAS BEEN CONSTANT

k = ANNUAL RATE OF DECLINE OF FERTILITY

CURRENT TOTAL FERTILITY

OFFICE OF POPULATION RESEARCH, PRINCETON UNIVERSITY

FIGURE 25. Ratio of the Birth Rate in a Population with a History of Fertility Declining at an Annual Rate k to the Stable Population Birth Rate, for Different Current Total Fertility and Values of k.

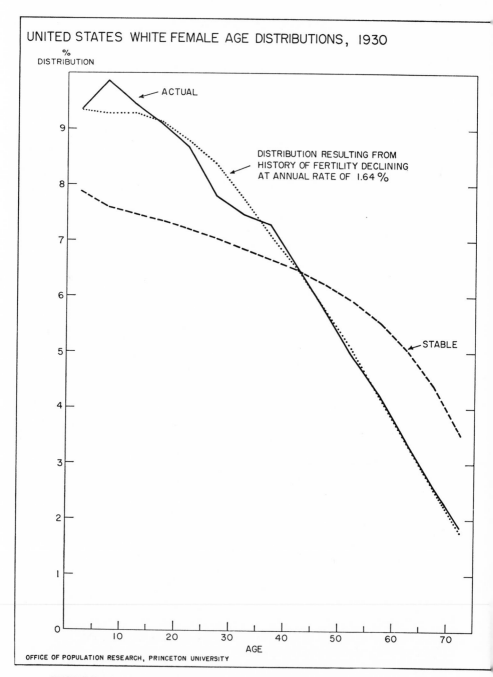

FIGURE 26. Age Distributions for the United States White Female Population, 1930: Actual, Stable, and Distribution Resulting from a History of Fertility Declining at Average Rate Observed in United States, 1910–1930.
Source: Table 17

age distribution in terms of the stable as follows:

$$(16) \qquad c_d(a) = K c_s(a) e^{-\frac{k}{2}a + \frac{k}{2A}a^2}$$

where K is a factor of proportionality such that

$$(17) \qquad \int_\alpha^\omega c_d(a)da = K \int_\alpha^\omega c_s(a) e^{-\frac{k}{2}a + \frac{k}{2A}a^2}da = 1$$

"Weighting" the stable age distribution by $e^{-\frac{k}{2}a + \frac{k}{2A}a^2}$ has the effect of reducing its total below one, and K (greater than one) must be inserted as a correcting factor. The greater the proportion of the aged in the stable population, the larger will be the factor required in Eq. (17). Since it is easily shown that K equals $\dfrac{b_d}{b_s}$—the ratio of the declining fertility birth rate to that of the stable population—we can see that a lengthy past history of declining fertility at a given annual rate has a bigger relative positive effect on the birth rate when fertility is low than when it is high. This relationship is illustrated in Figure 25 showing K—the ratio of the birth rate in a population with a history of fertility declining at an annual rate k to the stable population birth rate—for different current total fertility rates and annual rates of decrease of fertility.

The capacity of this rather abstract analysis to account for an actual age distribution is illustrated in Figure 26. Note that the actual age distribution of white females in 1930 is closely approximated by a completely synthetic distribution of the form:

$$c_d(a) = K c_s(a) e^{-\frac{k}{2}a + \frac{kA}{2}a^2}$$

The stable age distribution was calculated from the 1930 total fertility rate and a model life table with the same $\dot{e}_0$ as recorded for the white females in 1929–31; the value of k employed $(-.0164)$ was the average rate of decline of fertility 1910–1930. In other words, a close approximation of the actual 1930 white female age distribution can be calculated from three observed values—total fertility, its average rate of decline, and the expectation of life at birth.

Chapter 7. Adjusting for Age Heaping[1]

The number of persons listed at each age in a census can be erroneous because: (1) persons at different ages are differently subject to the likelihood of omission or erroneous inclusion in the census, and (2) persons are listed at incorrect ages. In this chapter, no attempt is made to detect omissions or erroneous inclusions.[2] Rather, its purpose is to adjust only for certain kinds of age misstatement—misstatement that takes the form of age heaping. Age heaping is the reporting of the age of a person at some conventionally preferred nearby number rather than the number reflecting his true age. For example, persons 59 or 61 (ages that are typically avoided) are often reported as 60 (a preferred age).

The adjustments for age heaping described in this chapter produce an age distribution in which the number at any given age is in an approximately appropriate relationship with neighboring age groups. Persons are reallocated to an age no more than five years removed from their reported age. Even an optimum adjustment for age heaping does not produce an age distribution free of the effects of age misstatement. Systematic tendencies toward over- and understatement of age, especially by large amounts, are not offset by age heaping adjustments. Thus the age distribution in most censuses has relatively too many persons at ages over 80 because of a common tendency for the aged to exaggerate their age. Adjustments for age heaping do not remove the effects of this tendency.[3]

THE USE OF AGE RATIOS

A concept of central importance in the method herein described to adjust for age heaping is that of age ratio. As here used, age ratio is defined as the number of persons at any age divided by the average number at the ten adjacent ages, five on each side.

[1] The material presented in this chapter represents a revised version of a previously published paper, Melvin Zelnik, "Age Heaping in the United States Census: 1880–1950," Milbank Memorial Fund *Quarterly*, Vol. XXXIX, No. 3 (July 1961), pp. 540–573.

[2] For estimates of undercounts, by age and sex, see Chapters 5 and 9.

[3] The estimates of under-enumeration by age and sex in Chapters 5 and 9 include the net effects of all forms of age misstatement.

If a population that neither gains nor loses members by migration is enumerated, the number recorded at each age is a consequence of four factors: (1) the number of births in each year preceding the count; (2) the number of deaths in each birth cohort from time of birth to time of enumeration; (3) age heaping and other forms of age misstatement; and (4) under- and/or over-enumeration of the population.[4] The fourth factor— to repeat—is outside the scope of this chapter. Age ratios calculated on the basis of a given age distribution will also be affected, in varying degrees, by these factors. If, over an eleven-year span, the number of births did not deviate from a linear trend, and if deaths did not cause a marked deviation from linearity, the age ratios of an accurately recorded age distribution would approximate unity; where deviations occurred, they would be the result of age heaping.[5] The rationale of our technique is to remove any nonlinearity introduced by an uneven birth sequence or by mortality, so that adjusted age ratios *will* reflect age heaping.

Age ratios were calculated for the native white males and native white females enumerated in each of the eight censuses from 1880 to 1950.[6] Ten ages were used in the calculation of the

---

[4] The native white population by definition cannot gain by foreign immigration. Emigration is of negligible importance except for the 1920 and 1950 censuses, owing to the size of the military forces overseas. For the various problems encountered in the several censuses, and the adjustments made to provide comparable populations, see Appendix A.

[5] It can easily be demonstrated that if a series of numbers is linear, the ratio of the mid-point of the series divided by the average of the ten adjacent numbers will be unity. If the correct age distribution is linear, then the age ratio will equal $\dfrac{n+r}{n-r/10}$, where n is the true number at the given age, and r is the number falsely reporting the age ($\dfrac{r}{10}$ is subtracted in the denominator because it is assumed that the persons erroneously reporting the given age are drawn from the adjacent ages).

[6] U.S. Census Office, 1880, *Statistics of the Population of the United States*, Table 20, pp. 548–550; *idem*, 1890, *Report on Population of the United States*, Part II, Table 1, pp. 2–5; *idem*, 1900, *Population*, Part II, Table xvi, pp. xxxvi–xxxix; U.S., Bureau of the Census: Population, General Report and Analysis, Table 29, in *1910 Census of Population*, Vol. I, pp. 310–313; *idem*, Population, General Report and Analytical Tables, Table 9, in *1920 Census of Population*, Vol. II, pp. 162–165; *idem*, General Report, Statistics by Subjects, Table 21, in *1930 Census of Population*, Vol. II, pp. 595–596; *idem*, Characteristics by Age, Part I (U.S. Summary), Table 3, in *1940 Census of Population*, Vol. IV, p. 13; *idem*, Characteristics of the Population, Part I (U.S. Summary), Table 94, in *1950 Census of Population*, Vol. II, pp. 1–165.

denominator of these ratios because: (1) an eleven-year interval was considered short enough to approximate a straight line and long enough to reduce the effect of annual fluctuations, and (2) the denominator for each age was composed of a series of ages ending in all other digits.[7]

The effect of mortality on the age ratios was estimated by the use of life tables. Age ratios were calculated for the "populations"[8] of different life tables widely separated in time.[9] The pattern of age ratios in the different life tables was remarkably similar. In all instances there was little deviation from linearity over eleven-year age-intervals in the range from age 10 to age 50. Age ratios differing sensibly from unity appeared only in childhood and above age 50.

Since the age ratios required must reflect only age heaping, and not deviate from unity because of mortality, correction for mortality was made in the census age ratios. The correction was simply a division of each census age ratio by the corresponding ratio for a life table population. A single set of corrections (the average ratio from life tables of 1901 and 1939–1941) was employed because of the remarkable similarity of the life table

[7] More accurately, the denominator for each age was composed of a series of ages in which eight digits appeared once and one digit twice. Age ratios for ages ending in 5 were calculated with a denominator containing two ages ending in 0. Since ages ending in 0 appear to be heavily preferred, at least for age 30 and over, there is a tendency to depress the age ratios for ages ending in 5. Similarly, there would be inflation of the age ratios for ages ending in 4 and 6, since the former has a double 9 in the denominator and the latter a double 1—in both instances a digit which is generally thought to be avoided. Since the over-preference for 0 seems to be largely at the expense of the two adjacent ages (those ending in 9 and 1), the average of the three would tend to approximate the "true" figure for each age.

On the basis of this reasoning, age ratios for ages ending in 4, 5, and 6 were calculated slightly differently from those of other ages. The numbers at ages ending in 9, 0, and 1 were averaged, and this average figure was then included in the denominator wherever the number at 9, 0, or 1 would have appeared. This correction is of negligible proportions and is included in the figures shown in Tables 6 and 7. Because of the small size of this correction, however, it did not seem warranted to correct the age ratios for ages ending in 0, which have a double 5 in the denominator (a digit which is less preferred than 0) or ages ending in 1, 2, 3, 7, 8, and 9.

[8] I.e., the $_1L_x$ columns of the life tables.

[9] For the females: U.S. Bureau of the Census, *United States Life Tables 1890, 1901, 1910 and 1901–1910*, prepared by James A. Glover, Table 21, pp. 92–93; idem, *United States Life Tables and Actuarial Tables 1939–1941*, prepared by Thomas N. E. Greville, Table 6, pp. 36–37.

For the males: *United States Life Tables 1890, 1901, 1910, and 1901–1910*, Table 19, pp. 90–91 and *United States Life Tables and Actuarial Tables 1939–1941*, Table 5, pp. 34–35.

age ratios. No adjustment was made if the life table age ratio differed from unity by less than .005.

The ideal basis for testing the validity of the assumption of the linearity of births (and for correcting where invalid) would be an annual series of birth statistics for the United States beginning about 1850. The unavailability of these figures required an alternative approach to the problem.[10] The method that has been used to correct for the provisional assumption of the linearity of births depends instead on the identification of large and small birth cohorts (relative to their neighbors) at points in time some years after birth. More explicitly, cohort size was established from its effect on the age ratios calculated from the enumerated populations in a series of censuses.

THE LINEAR TREND IN AGE HEAPING

Tables 6 and 7 show a decrease, for each sex, in the average deviation (the mean of absolute deviations from unity) of the age ratios for each successive census, 1880 to 1950, if 1900 is ignored.[11] When the age ratios for each year of age are plotted, they appear to be approaching unity in a linear fashion[12] with the exception in most instances of 1900 (Figures 27 to 36). It was therefore assumed, on the basis of this evidence, that the

---

[10] An early attempt, before this study reached its present magnitude, was made to use the birth statistics available for individual states back to the mid-1800's. The limitations of these data are described in Chapter 1, pp. 1–2. The shortcomings in the data made them non-usable for this purpose.

[11] The 1900 census asked not only "age at last birthday" but also "date of birth," the only time (prior to the 1960 census) this information has been requested in a United States census. All available evidence seems to suggest a higher degree of accuracy in the 1900 age distributions resulting from the inclusion of this question. See Allyn A. Young, "Age," *Supplementary Analysis and Derivative Tables, Twelfth Census of the United States,* U.S., Bureau of the Census, 1900, pp. 130–174. There is also some evidence to indicate that the inclusion of this question ("date of birth") in the 1960 census has had the effect of changing long-standing patterns of age misreporting aside from any change in the degree of accuracy of age reporting; see Chapters 5 and 9.

[12] It was at this point that it became apparent that the method being used to adjust the native white populations would not be applicable to the non-whites. The life table adjusted age ratios for them are clearly curvilinear; this meant that more complicated methods would be needed, assuming that the problem was even solveable. No attempt has been made to work out an alternative technique of adjusting for age heaping which would be applicable to the nonwhites

There is also some evidence to indicate that the time pattern of age heaping for certain ages of the native whites (up to and including the 1950 census) is curvilinear rather than linear; see below, pp. 124–126.

TABLE 6

Age Ratios[a] for Census Enumerated Native White Males, Ages 5–85,
1880–1950, Adjusted by Life Table Age Ratios

| | Census | | | | | | | | Life |
Age	1880	1890	1900	1910	1920	1930	1940	1950	Table
5	1.035	1.038	1.020	1.014	1.042	1.058	1.009	.943	.991
6	1.052	1.079	1.038	1.016	1.021	1.033	.937	.990	1.000
7	.983	.988	1.021	.981	1.003	1.001	.944	1.055	1.000
8	1.015	.999	1.028	.978	1.007	1.061	.997	.983	1.000
9	.958	.934	.983	.952	.974	1.032	.988	.950	1.000
10	1.085	1.039	1.036	.990	1.024	1.010	1.024	.949	1.000
11	.931	.894	.966	.923	.992	.958	.972	.944	1.000
12	1.108	1.066	.994	1.040	1.072	1.042	1.053	.998	1.000
13	.984	.954	.968	.978	.988	.977	1.011	.976	1.000
14	.998	1.065	1.005	1.043	1.021	1.027	1.019	.972	1.000
15	.841	.956	.996	.968	.929	.989	1.014	.968	1.000
16	.894	1.042	1.025	1.047	1.006	1.020	1.034	.943	1.000
17	.913	.971	.994	1.020	.969	1.009	1.003	.959	1.000
18	1.067	1.053	.996	1.050	.998	1.023	1.075	1.000	1.000
19	1.033	.976	.952	.980	.986	.996	1.028	.988	1.000
20	1.033	.912	.976	.966	.922	.966	.971	.986	1.000
21	1.098	1.111	1.006	1.034	1.024	1.037	1.015	1.027	1.000
22	1.070	1.052	1.018	.990	1.002	1.015	.975	1.000	1.000
23	1.035	1.052	1.007	.999	.998	1.005	.983	1.004	1.000
24	1.026	.992	1.040	1.016	1.024	1.005	1.014	.998	1.000
25	1.037	.922	1.033	1.004	1.012	.976	1.004	1.048	1.000
26	.974	.886	.982	1.006	1.021	.975	1.001	1.010	1.000
27	.920	.901	.999	.968	1.031	.948	1.004	.995	1.000
28	1.047	1.095	1.034	1.062	1.056	.982	1.022	1.051	1.000
29	.858	.935	.949	.933	.967	1.016	1.010	1.021	1.000
30	1.307	1.349	1.181	1.138	1.051	1.105	1.051	1.046	1.000
31	.748	.823	.871	.812	.868	.864	.916	.959	1.000
32	.972	1.010	1.005	1.006	.963	1.011	1.054	1.000	1.000
33	.909	.960	.961	.931	.948	.945	.978	.967	1.000
34	.886	.932	.930	.998	1.016	.980	1.018	1.010	1.000
35	1.235	1.180	.995	1.126	1.112	1.092	1.039	1.048	1.000
36	.964	.971	.875	.977	1.008	1.000	.960	.998	1.000
37	.859	.898	.907	.934	.966	.979	.920	.992	1.000
38	1.035	1.063	1.108	1.113	1.076	1.089	.972	1.022	1.000
39	.911	.889	1.071	.979	.988	.985	1.057	1.009	1.000
40	1.405	1.313	1.230	1.222	1.102	1.144	1.111	1.077	1.000
41	.709	.780	.899	.816	.811	.850	.860	.934	1.000
42	.982	.994	1.029	1.085	1.053	1.078	1.075	1.090	1.000
43	.859	.881	.932	.915	.937	.919	.972	.993	1.000
44	.882	.834	.960	.871	.882	.920	.939	.944	1.000
45	1.269	1.245	1.116	1.057	1.130	1.122	1.058	1.021	1.000
46	.932	.980	.916	.816	1.003	.940	.967	.948	1.000
47	.908	.897	.930	.877	1.008	.935	1.013	.947	1.000
48	.985	.990	.967	1.085	1.024	1.023	1.031	.951	1.000
49	.888	.864	.963	1.046	1.001	.982	.986	1.078	1.000

(CONTINUED)

94

TABLE 6 (CONCLUDED)

				Census					Life
Age	1880	1890	1900	1910	1920	1930	1940	1950	Table
50	1.412	1.356	1.202	1.303	1.212	1.181	1.127	1.102	1.000
51	.756	.766	.910	.872	.840	.821	.897	.882	1.000
52	1.097	1.047	1.039	1.136	1.107	1.081	1.067	1.028	1.000
53	.950	.987	.945	.956	.968	.974	.947	.983	1.000
54	.950	.982	.959	.995	.926	1.033	1.001	1.014	1.005
55	1.090	1.017	1.065	1.013	.896	1.004	.985	.983	1.005
56	1.004	1.030	.981	.987	.908	.983	.993	1.000	1.006
57	.831	.942	.908	.888	.883	.943	.937	1.007	1.006
58	.933	.937	.910	.949	1.044	1.004	1.019	1.016	1.006
59	.861	.781	.937	.916	1.021	.967	.991	.968	1.006
60	1.408	1.338	1.146	1.153	1.222	1.186	1.063	1.065	1.007
61	.779	.746	.824	.801	.852	.817	.820	.893	1.007
62	1.049	1.006	.995	1.020	1.057	1.033	.982	.975	1.008
63	1.002	1.060	1.030	1.005	1.064	1.026	1.008	.966	1.008
64	.944	.961	.984	.957	.958	.924	1.044	.988	1.009
65	1.176	1.186	1.039	1.165	1.121	1.049	1.145	1.152	1.009
66	.883	.921	.987	.912	.860	.786	.907	.951	1.009
67	.879	.916	1.010	.913	.918	.891	.992	.984	1.009
68	.995	.952	.935	.953	.932	1.049	.984	.966	1.009
69	.933	.823	.933	.982	.973	1.066	.977	.954	1.009
70	1.226	1.291	1.066	1.073	1.055	1.139	1.087	1.002	1.008
71	.803	.814	.847	.792	.826	.896	.885	.868	1.008
72	1.003	1.065	1.017	1.029	1.026	1.068	1.038	1.034	1.007
73	.965	.975	.980	.974	.943	.980	.989	1.002	1.006
74	.950	.960	.973	.984	.974	.971	.944	1.023	1.000
75	1.044	1.052	1.044	1.031	1.115	1.033	.914	1.049	1.000
76	.959	.951	.942	.991	.950	.922	.855	.959	1.000
77	.851	.860	.946	.916	.895	.868	.865	.940	.991
78	.930	1.050	.955	.944	.902	.928	1.043	.990	.984
79	1.018	.846	.956	.923	.965	.944	1.074	.965	.976
80	1.286	1.201	1.053	.984	.943	.989	1.065	1.069	.965
81	.765	.828	.933	.813	.816	.847	.932	.895	.952
82	.885	1.000	.972	1.001	.970	.950	1.002	1.001	.937
83	.896	.952	.924	.965	.992	.955	.982	1.009	.920
84	.946	1.037	.978	1.024	1.003	.987	1.003	.997	.901
85	.883	.927	.914	.934	.910	.964	.903	.868	.879
Average Deviation	.107	.097	.054	.066	.061	.057	.046	.038	

SOURCES: The census age ratios have been calculated from the 1880–1950 enumerated native white populations (see footnote 6, p. 91). The life table age ratios are the average of the age ratios calculated from the $_1L_x$ values of the 1901 and 1939–1941 life tables (see footnote 9, p. 92).

^{a} Age Ratio = $\dfrac{\text{Number at any age}}{\text{Average of ten adjacent ages}}$.

TABLE 7

Age Ratios[a] for Census Enumerated Native White Females, Ages 5–85,
1880–1950, Adjusted by Life Table Age Ratios

	Census								Life
Age	1880	1890	1900	1910	1920	1930	1940	1950	Table
5	1.041	1.047	1.019	1.013	1.037	1.049	1.006	.943	.992
6	1.062	1.093	1.043	1.025	1.026	1.035	.936	.989	1.000
7	.994	.988	1.020	.983	1.005	1.004	.951	1.059	1.000
8	1.016	1.007	1.031	.980	1.013	1.068	.997	.986	1.000
9	.955	.932	.979	.947	.973	1.025	.983	.951	1.000
10	1.057	1.012	1.032	.986	1.022	1.011	1.020	.953	1.000
11	.939	.894	.968	.928	.995	.968	.979	.945	1.000
12	1.083	1.051	.990	1.029	1.057	1.028	1.041	.992	1.000
13	.976	.949	.965	.976	.985	.978	1.010	.973	1.000
14	.969	1.032	.990	1.022	1.002	1.010	1.007	.956	1.000
15	.847	.968	.995	.967	.938	.982	1.006	.962	1.000
16	.933	1.077	1.030	1.060	1.017	1.023	1.031	.930	1.000
17	.916	.962	.992	.998	.963	.990	.987	.945	1.000
18	1.156	1.116	1.022	1.089	1.009	1.043	1.086	1.002	1.000
19	1.018	.943	.967	.967	.971	.995	1.025	1.004	1.000
20	1.146	1.072	1.021	1.035	.969	1.008	1.000	1.002	1.000
21	.961	.958	.946	.963	.963	1.004	1.008	1.015	1.000
22	1.102	1.070	1.027	1.012	1.017	1.030	.988	.999	1.000
23	1.012	1.008	1.017	1.008	1.028	1.006	.992	.996	1.000
24	1.028	.989	1.052	1.022	1.040	1.009	1.010	1.001	1.000
25	1.065	.984	1.062	1.053	1.056	1.013	1.025	1.065	1.000
26	.961	.911	.981	1.012	1.026	.985	1.009	1.025	1.000
27	.866	.877	.984	.931	.981	.932	.988	.994	1.000
28	1.040	1.102	1.015	1.061	1.055	.987	1.028	1.052	1.000
29	.814	.896	.934	.893	.930	.985	.995	1.012	1.000
30	1.310	1.358	1.155	1.158	1.135	1.127	1.078	1.064	1.000
31	.711	.786	.875	.798	.856	.846	.902	.943	1.000
32	.992	1.038	1.008	1.033	1.010	1.023	1.064	1.020	1.000
33	.903	.947	.959	.925	.926	.945	.965	.970	1.000
34	.896	.928	.936	.984	.959	.978	1.000	.993	1.000
35	1.227	1.138	.985	1.116	1.111	1.096	1.036	1.052	1.000
36	1.004	.979	.893	.995	1.000	1.010	.970	1.010	1.000
37	.888	.880	.919	.926	.911	.960	.917	.980	1.000
38	1.074	1.067	1.104	1.121	1.105	1.115	1.000	1.031	1.000
39	.886	.868	1.071	.952	.972	.961	1.033	.998	1.000
40	1.436	1.350	1.207	1.251	1.175	1.174	1.148	1.108	1.000
41	.684	.731	.886	.789	.779	.815	.833	.907	1.000
42	.999	1.008	1.030	1.081	1.079	1.079	1.073	1.088	1.000
43	.882	.891	.954	.920	.947	.924	.961	.987	1.000
44	.920	.895	.970	.877	.928	.921	.941	.931	1.000
45	1.233	1.239	1.070	1.043	1.137	1.113	1.060	1.023	1.000
46	.904	.951	.908	.830	.909	.934	.964	.939	1.000
47	.890	.896	.932	.886	.946	.924	.993	.939	1.000
48	1.023	1.047	.989	1.134	1.053	1.064	1.063	.976	1.000
49	.873	.861	.972	1.040	.987	.965	.970	1.057	1.000

(CONTINUED)

96

TABLE 7 (CONCLUDED)

Age	Census								Life Table
	1880	1890	1900	1910	1920	1930	1940	1950	
50	1.492	1.459	1.204	1.335	1.293	1.230	1.175	1.163	1.000
51	.714	.728	.880	.825	.813	.795	.864	.859	1.000
52	1.039	1.012	.991	1.078	1.064	1.051	1.053	1.025	1.000
53	.901	.918	.920	.925	.928	.946	.932	.963	1.000
54	.982	1.013	.980	1.014	.943	1.039	1.005	1.008	1.000
55	1.103	1.042	1.081	1.020	.934	1.035	1.010	1.002	1.000
56	1.000	1.034	1.000	.972	.905	.962	.975	.987	1.000
57	.815	.881	.933	.865	.885	.925	.931	.996	1.000
58	.967	.964	.948	.984	1.089	1.034	1.046	1.039	1.005
59	.841	.782	.959	.912	1.015	.953	.973	.975	1.005
60	1.512	1.436	1.193	1.241	1.282	1.250	1.124	1.103	1.006
61	.721	.705	.819	.767	.816	.798	.808	.872	1.007
62	1.006	.970	.975	.986	1.019	1.012	.967	.963	1.008
63	.955	1.013	1.012	.976	1.028	.993	.986	.957	1.008
64	.936	.971	.985	.967	.957	.918	1.017	.958	1.009
65	1.213	1.240	1.064	1.196	1.136	1.088	1.202	1.211	1.009
66	.886	.918	.978	.924	.860	.798	.904	.952	1.010
67	.880	.898	.967	.917	.884	.878	.966	.966	1.010
68	1.007	.970	.932	.998	.966	1.076	1.005	.999	1.011
69	.886	.803	.932	.938	.956	1.045	.968	.940	1.011
70	1.332	1.352	1.112	1.138	1.122	1.191	1.138	1.065	1.012
71	.728	.744	.816	.754	.791	.844	.842	.841	1.012
72	.990	1.019	1.000	1.019	1.002	1.047	1.020	1.012	1.012
73	.943	.946	.943	.958	.931	.960	.966	.988	1.012
74	.958	.944	.973	.965	.960	.945	.914	.999	1.011
75	1.120	1.108	1.080	1.074	1.155	1.076	.975	1.085	1.009
76	.972	.948	.941	.999	.960	.925	.863	.960	1.006
77	.846	.871	.929	.897	.902	.852	.856	.913	1.000
78	.931	1.017	.938	.942	.935	.920	1.037	.980	1.000
79	.906	.815	.926	.883	.950	.916	1.037	.949	.991
80	1.340	1.228	1.092	1.037	1.005	1.044	1.126	1.106	.982
81	.712	.792	.887	.773	.790	.824	.897	.880	.972
82	.917	.972	.950	.986	.976	.960	.995	.999	.960
83	.897	.970	.924	.969	1.005	.950	.983	.989	.946
84	1.068	1.084	.976	1.048	1.024	.996	.985	.971	.930
85	.954	1.004	.923	.976	.944	.979	.932	.895	.912
Average Deviation	.118	.106	.058	.076	.070	.066	.051	.045	

SOURCES: The census age ratios have been calculated from the 1880–1950 enumerated native white populations (see footnote 6, p. 91). The life table age ratios are the average of the age ratios calculated from the $_1L_x$ values of the 1901 and 1939–1941 life tables (see footnote 9, p. 92).

^{a} Age Ratio $= \dfrac{\text{Number at any age}}{\text{Average of ten adjacent ages}}$.

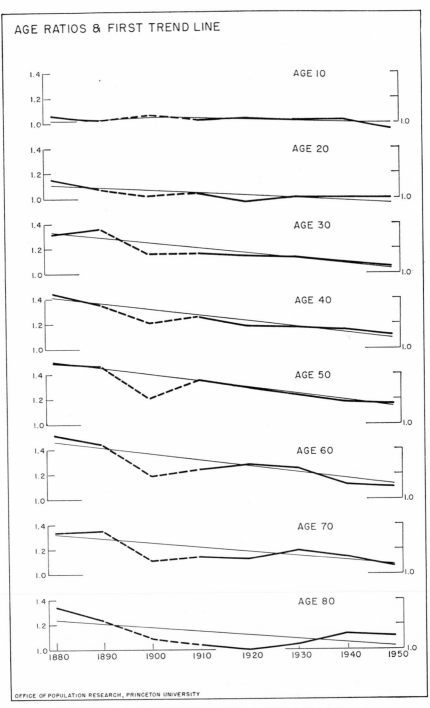

FIGURE 27.   Trend Lines Fitted to Age Ratios of Enumerated
Native White Females, 1880–1950: Ages Ending in 0.

Source: Table 7

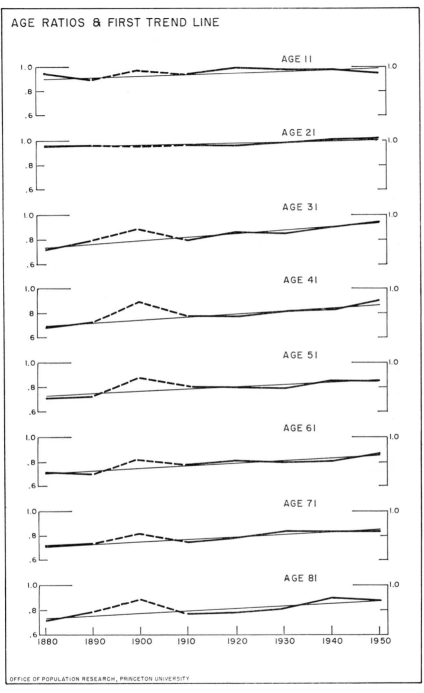

FIGURE 28.   Trend Lines Fitted to Age Ratios of Enumerated
Native White Females, 1880–1950: Ages Ending in 1.
Source: Table 7

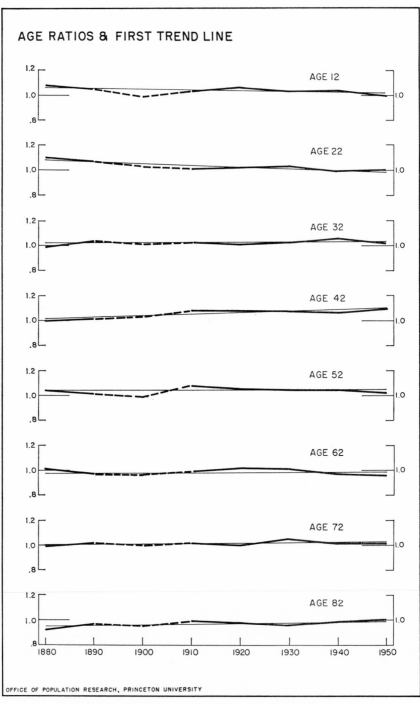

FIGURE 29.   Trend Lines Fitted to Age Ratios of Enumerated
Native White Females, 1880–1950: Ages Ending in 2.

Source: Table 7

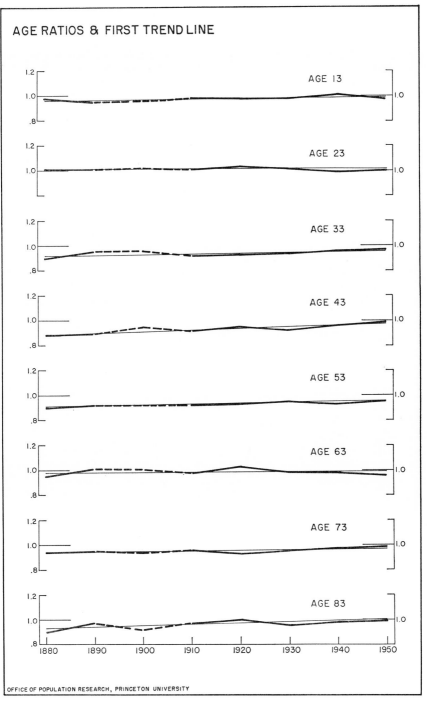

FIGURE 30. Trend Lines Fitted to Age Ratios of Enumerated
Native White Females, 1880–1950: Ages Ending in 3.
Source: Table 7

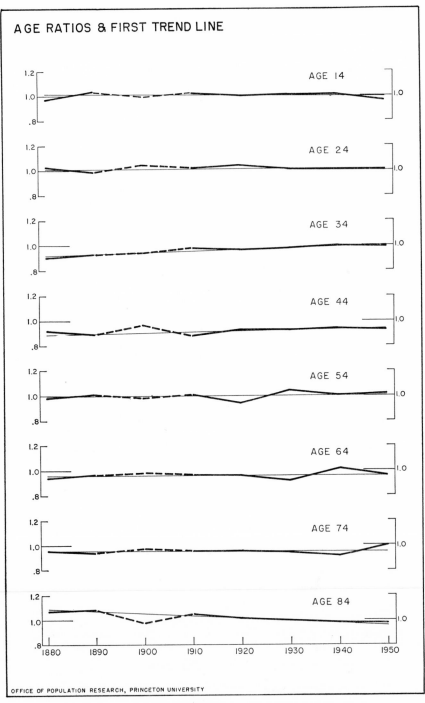

FIGURE 31.   Trend Lines Fitted to Age Ratios of Enumerated
Native White Females, 1880–1950: Ages Ending in 4.

Source: Table 7

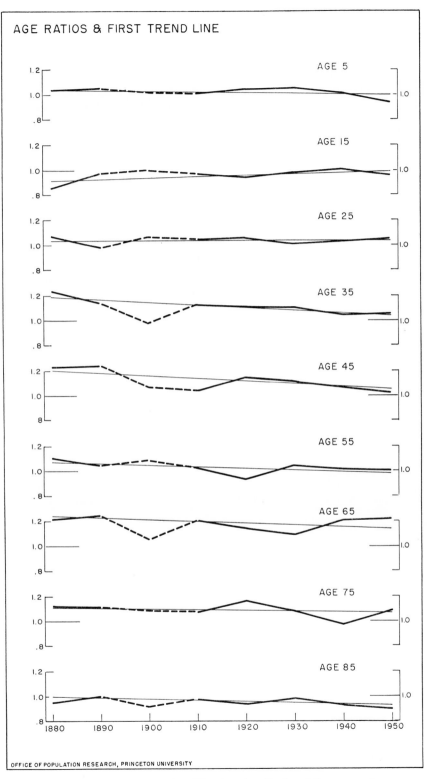

FIGURE 32. Trend Lines Fitted to Age Ratios of Enumerated
Native White Females, 1880–1950: Ages Ending in 5.

Source: Table 7

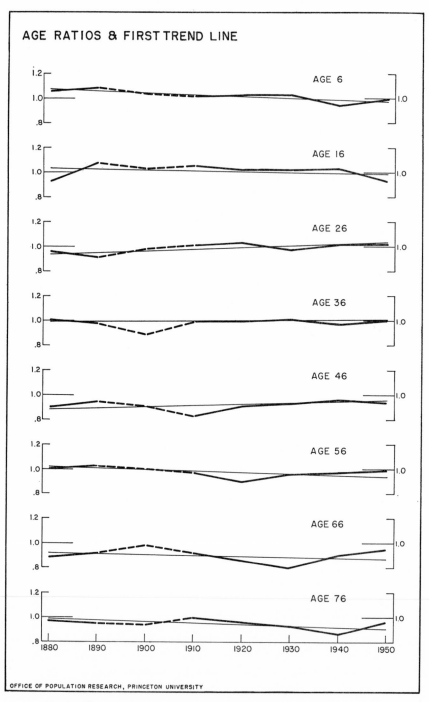

FIGURE 33.   Trend Lines Fitted to Age Ratios of Enumerated
Native White Females, 1880–1950: Ages Ending in 6.
Source: Table 7

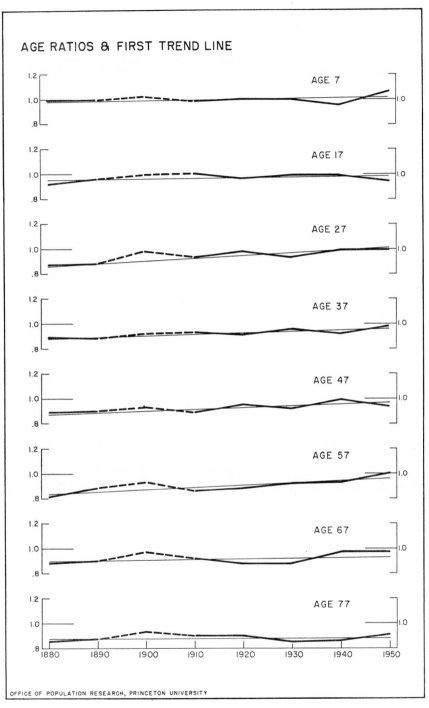

AGE RATIOS & FIRST TREND LINE

AGE 7

AGE 17

AGE 27

AGE 37

AGE 47

AGE 57

AGE 67

AGE 77

FIGURE 34.   Trend Lines Fitted to Age Ratios of Enumerated
Native White Females, 1880–1950: Ages Ending in 7.
Source: Table 7

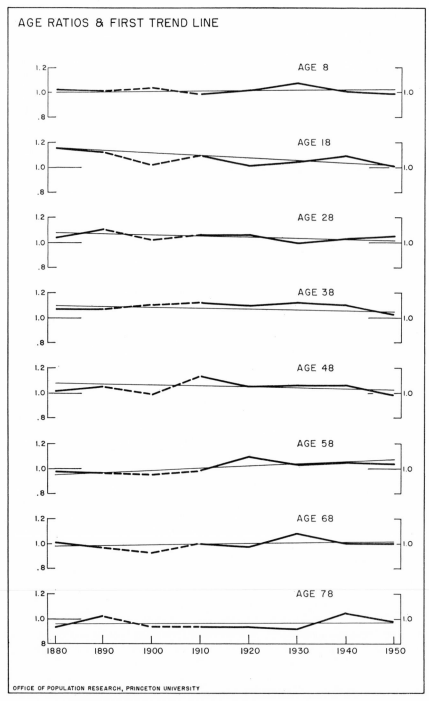

FIGURE 35.   Trend Lines Fitted to Age Ratios of Enumerated
Native White Females, 1880–1950: Ages Ending in 8.
Source: Table 7

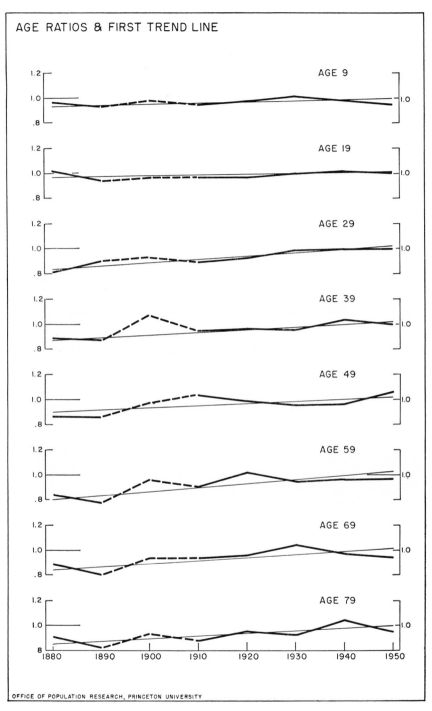

FIGURE 36.   Trend Lines Fitted to Age Ratios of Enumerated
Native White Females, 1880–1950: Ages Ending in 9.
Source: Table 7

age ratios for each age were, through time, changing in a linear fashion (again, with the noted exception of 1900) with deviations from the trend caused primarily by birth cohorts of unusual size. For each age a trend line of age ratios was established by connecting the average of the 1880, 1890, and 1910 values with the average of 1920, 1930, 1940, and 1950 values.[13] These average age ratios were centered on 1893⅓ and 1935 respectively; intermediate censal values were estimated by simple interpolation while values for censuses beyond these points were arrived at by simple extrapolation (Figures 27 to 36).

PRELIMINARY ESTIMATES OF DEVIANT SIZE OF COHORT

The true size of a birth cohort relative to its neighbors remains very nearly constant through time (except perhaps for certain ages of males through decimation of a cohort by war losses). A cohort of unusual size should therefore appear as a deviation from the trend line each time the cohort is enumerated. Thus the birth cohort of 1864 can easily be traced through time by its appearance as a deviation from eight separate trend lines (representing eight ages) from 1880 when it was age 15 to 1940 when it was age 75 (Figure 32). If the trend lines represent the degree of age heaping, the deviations from the trend lines reflect the size of the birth cohorts. The size of the deviations does not remain constant because of random elements, and consequently the average deviation was considered to be the best indication of the deviant size of the birth cohort.

The deviations of each birth cohort from the various trend lines, as the cohort moves through time and is enumerated at an age approximately 10 years older in each census,[14] were totaled and averaged; this average figure may be considered the deviation of the age ratios from the trend line due to cohort size. Because of the non-consistency of the 1900 census with the general assumption of linearity in age heaping, the deviations of the cohorts enumerated in 1900 were not included in estimating the average size of the cohort.

---

[13] Since 1900 obviously does not fit the trend of age heaping, it would be incorrect to include it for the establishment of the trend line.

[14] For the way in which the problems arising from the differences in census dates were handled, see Appendix A.

Adjusted Trend Lines and Final Estimates of Deviant Size of Cohorts

The trend lines themselves, however, were influenced by the size of the cohort. In other words, the age ratios used to determine the trend lines reflect both age heaping and the relative size of the birth cohort. An estimate of cohort size based on these trend lines will not be a true measure of actual (relative) cohort size but may be considered a first approximation to it. Consequently, a correction factor was derived, reflecting the influence of the cohort size on the trend lines, and applied to the average cohort deviation.[15] This corrected cohort deviation (which is the first approximation to the relative size of the birth cohort) was used to adjust the age ratios, taking into account the differences in census date.

The age ratios corrected by the size of the cohort (or at least a first approximation to it) may be considered a "more pure" measure of age heaping, and trend lines based on these corrected age ratios a more accurate representation of the true trend. Also, the differences between unadjusted age ratios and trend

---

[15] If the cohort size is known to deviate from a linear sequence of cohorts by an amount d, then one end of the preliminary trend line of age heaping is raised by $\dfrac{d}{n_i}$ where n_i represents the number of age ratios used in establishing that end of the trend line i. Consequently, the observed deviation from the ith trend line will tend to be smaller than d by an amount $\dfrac{d}{n_i}$.

Let n_i = number of age ratios determining position of one end of trend line i
N = number of times a cohort is observed
d' = estimated deviant size of cohort as determined by the average of the deviations from the several original trend lines
d = true deviant size of cohort

then $\dfrac{\sum \dfrac{d}{n_i}}{N} = \dfrac{\text{sum of effects when affected}}{\text{number of times observed}} =$ the error in estimating the average deviation in cohort size because of the distorting effect this cohort has on each of the several trend lines it helps determine. If this error is rd, then $d' = d - rd$, or $d = \dfrac{d'}{(1 - r)}$; and since

$$r = \frac{\sum \dfrac{1}{n_i}}{N}, \quad d = \frac{d'}{1 - \dfrac{\sum \dfrac{1}{n_i}}{N}}$$

lines established on the basis of the cohort-adjusted age ratios provide a more accurate measure of the size of the cohort.

Because of this reasoning, new trend lines were calculated from the cohort-adjusted age ratios.[16] These new trend lines, following the original assumption of linearity in age heaping, are the final basis for our estimate of the degree of age heaping for each year of age at each census, with the exception of 1900.

If this procedure is valid, then the age ratios, corrected by adjustment for cohort size, should agree very closely with the second trend line values. The "closeness of fit" between these two measures is shown in Figures 37 to 46. While not perfect, it can be seen that there is a high degree of improvement (compare with Figures 27 to 36) and a relatively good agreement.

POSSIBLE CHANGES IN AGE HEAPING AS A RESULT OF OLD AGE ASSISTANCE

An attempt was made to take account of the effect of old age assistance legislation enacted in the 1930's on patterns of age heaping. It appears that ages 60–64 were relatively understated in 1940 and 1950, whereas ages 65–69 were heavily overstated (see Chapter 5) with the persons under 65 reporting themselves at the latter ages so as to be eligible to receive old age benefits. Since the legislation affected the 1940 and 1950 censuses, age heaping for these ages in these two censuses would not follow the linear trend originally assumed to exist. The pattern would instead be curvilinear. For ages 62–68 (where presumably the bulk of the change would occur) therefore, the second end of each trend line was determined by averaging the values of 1910, 1920, and 1930 and centering it on 1920. Values after this date were determined by extrapolation. The average relative size of each cohort was then determined in the same manner as explained in the text except that the deviations for ages 62–68 in 1940 and 1950 were not included in the estimation. In this respect these ages were treated in a fashion similar to the way in which 1900 was treated.

[16] Since every cohort had to be enumerated at least twice to estimate its size, it was not possible to adjust the age ratios for ages 5–14 in 1950 and 75–85 in 1880. The second trend lines for ages 5–14 were thus arrived at by averaging the 1920, 1930, and 1940 figures, centering it on 1930; for ages 75–85, the left side of the trend line was the average of 1890 and 1910, centered on 1900. For all other ages, the procedure used was the same as in determining the first trend lines.

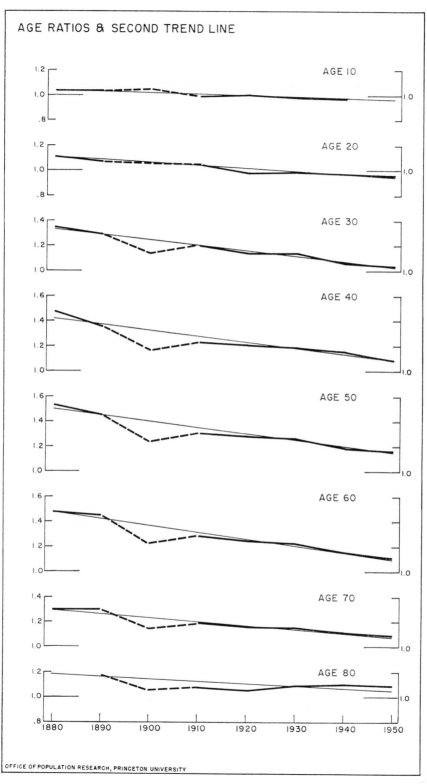

FIGURE 37. Final Trend Lines and Age Ratios Adjusted f or Cohort
Size, Native White Females, 1880–1950: Ages Ending in 0.

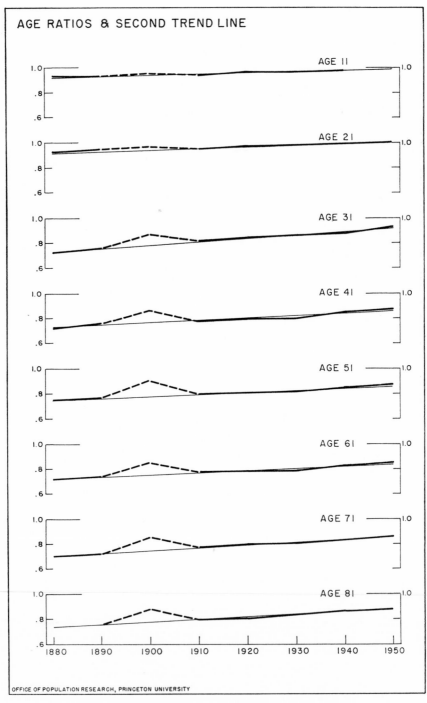

FIGURE 38. Final Trend Lines and Age Ratios Adjusted for Cohort Size, Native White Females, 1880–1950: Ages Ending in 1.

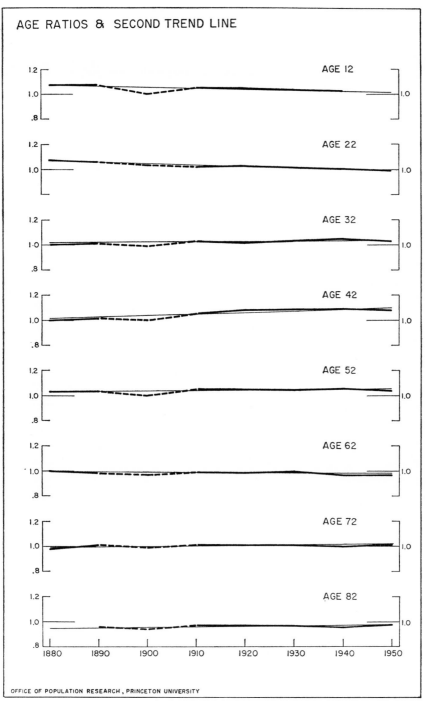

FIGURE 39.   Final Trend Lines and Age Ratios Adjusted for Cohort Size, Native White Females, 1880–1950: Ages Ending in 2.

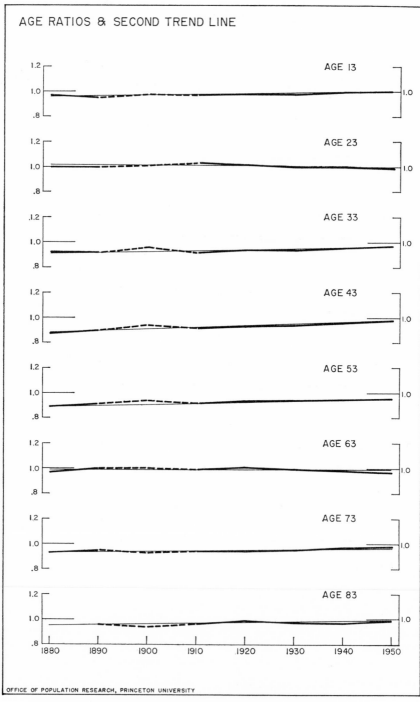

AGE RATIOS & SECOND TREND LINE

AGE 13

AGE 23

AGE 33

AGE 43

AGE 53

AGE 63

AGE 73

AGE 83

FIGURE 40.   Final Trend Lines and Age Ratios Adjusted for Cohort
Size, Native White Females, 1880–1950: Ages Ending in 3.

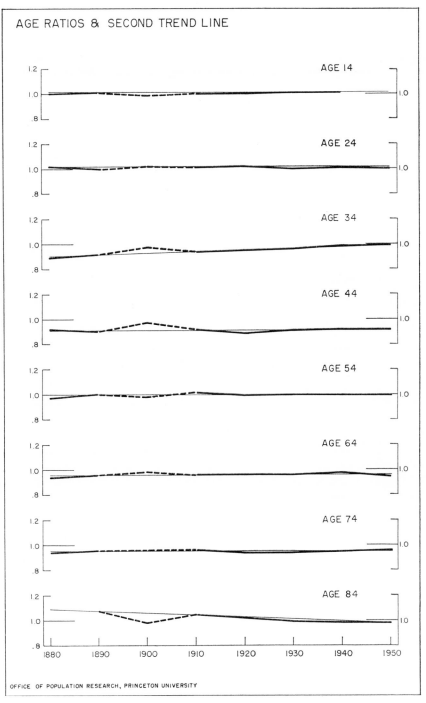

FIGURE 41.   Final Trend Lines and Age Ratios Adjusted for Cohort
Size, Native White Females, 1880–1950: Ages Ending in 4.

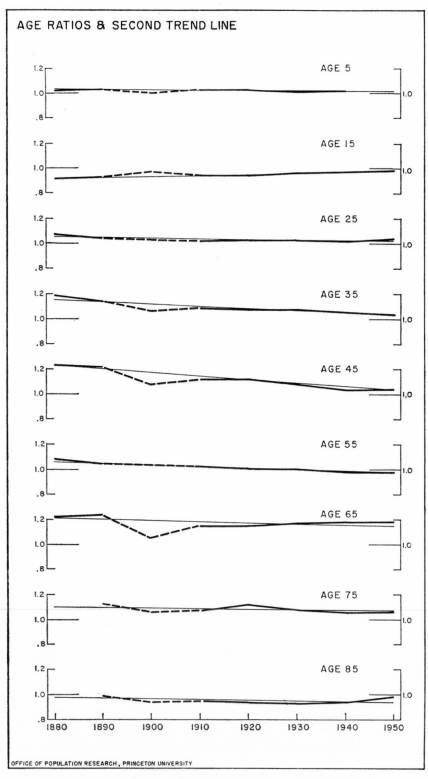

FIGURE 42.   Final Trend Lines and Age Ratios Adjusted for Cohort Size, Native White Females, 1880–1950: Ages Ending in 5.

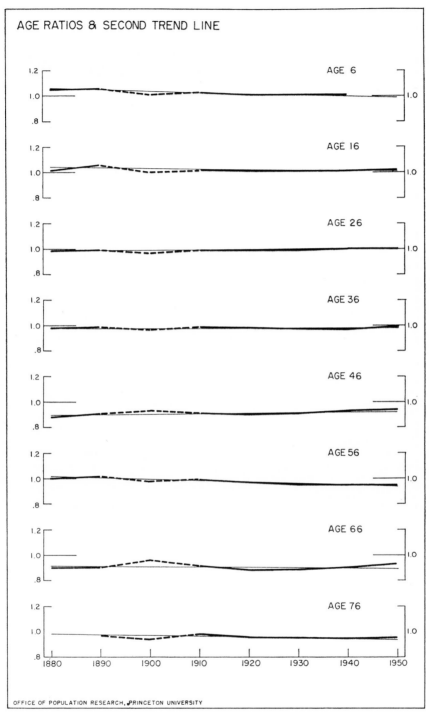

FIGURE 43.   Final Trend Lines and Age Ratios Adjusted for Cohort
Size, Native White Females, 1880–1950: Ages Ending in 6.

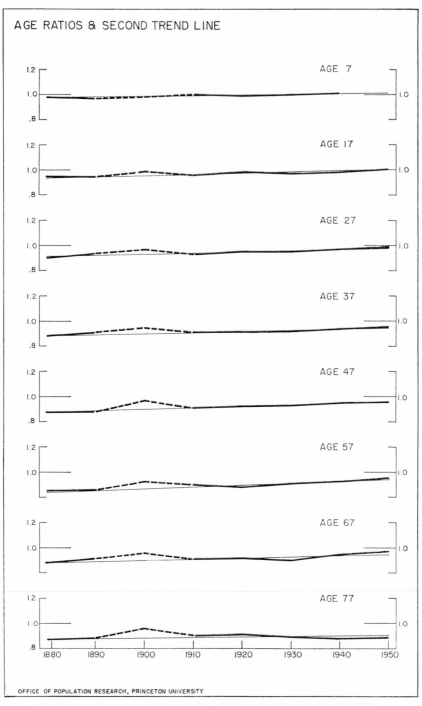

FIGURE 44.   Final Trend Lines and Age Ratios Adjusted for Cohort
Size, Native White Females, 1880–1950: Ages Ending in 7.

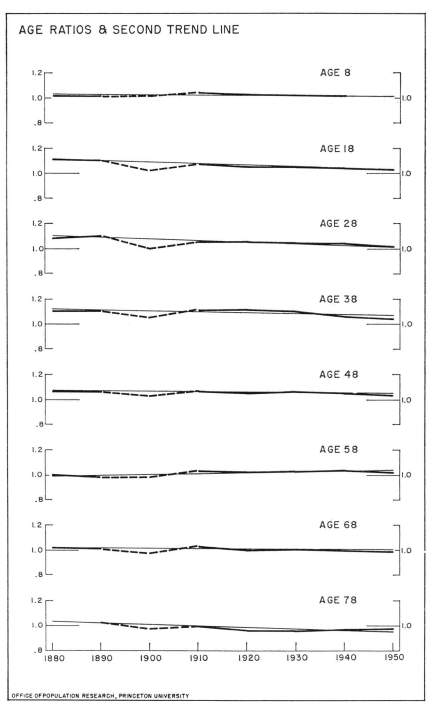

FIGURE 45. Final Trend Lines and Age Ratios Adjusted for Cohort Size, Native White Females, 1880–1950: Ages Ending in 8.

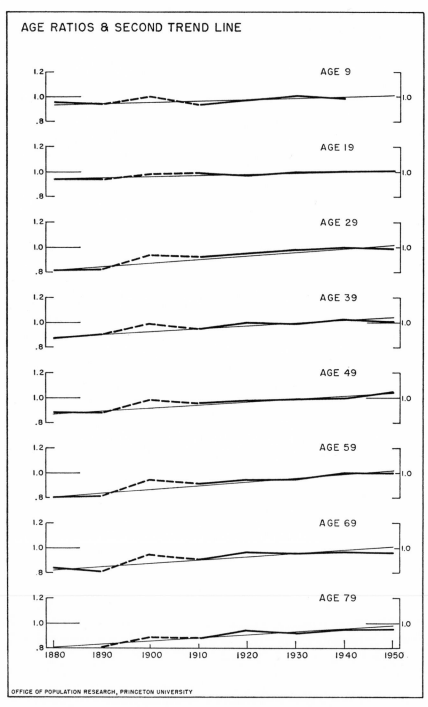

FIGURE 46.   Final Trend Lines and Age Ratios Adjusted for Cohort Size, Native White Females, 1880–1950: Ages Ending in 9.

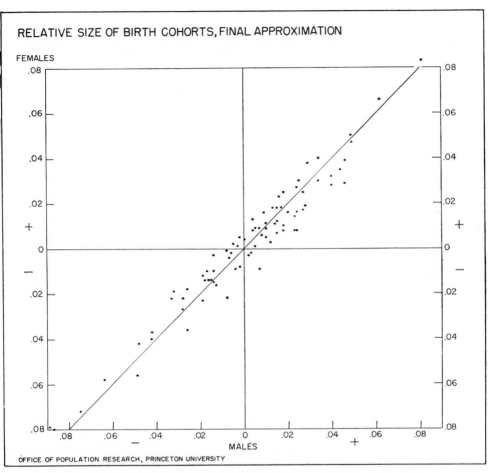

FIGURE 47. Scattergram of Average Relative Size of Birth Cohorts for White Males and Females as Estimated from Final Trend Lines of Age Heaping, 1850–1934.

After adjusting the age ratios for cohort size and plotting the cohort-adjusted values, certain features were revealed which threw doubt on this alternative attempt. First, the closeness of fit between these values and their trend lines was not as good as had been the case when these ages had not been treated differently from the other ages.

Secondly, for some ages, the divergence from the linear trend was as large, or almost as large, in 1930 as in 1940 and 1950, and

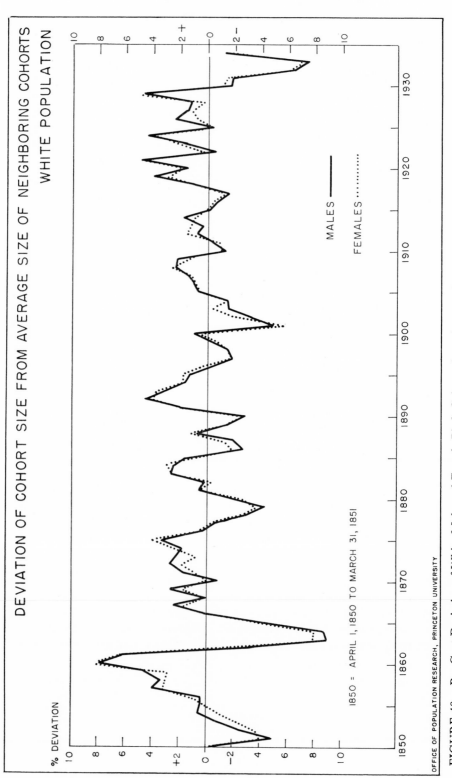

FIGURE 48. Per Cent Deviation of White Male and Female Birth Cohorts from Average Size of Ten Neighboring Birth Cohorts, 1850–1934.

the old age assistance legislation was not enacted until the middle 1930's. Thirdly, for certain ages, notably 64 and 68 (for both sexes), the cohort-adjusted age ratios went in a direction opposite to what one would expect: age 64 showed an increase in heaping while age 68 showed a decrease. Thus, the effect on age reporting of the social security legislation that is conspicuous in a changed pattern of under-enumeration does not show up as might be expected in single-year age heaping.

THE USE OF AGE HEAPING ESTIMATES IN ESTIMATING THE ACTUAL SIZE OF COHORTS

Theoretically the relative size of each birth cohort should be the same for both sexes, i.e., the correlation between the relative size of birth cohorts as estimated for males and females should be 1.000. A scatter diagram of these two series (Figure 47) shows that the correlation, while not unity, is extremely high (0.97). The deviations present can possibly be attributed to random elements in age heaping, to the effects of under-enumeration of one sex as compared to the other, or to the effects of war losses on the males.

Figure 48 shows these estimates of the relative size of the birth cohorts plotted against time. This diagram illustrates mainly three points: (1) as mentioned, the close correlation between the male and female series; (2) the large dips and rises in the births at periods when they would be expected (e.g., the hollow during the Civil War and the small size of the 1930 cohorts); and (3) the fluctuations in births as far back as the 1850's instead of the relatively even progression one might have expected.

These estimates of birth cohorts, while providing some confirmation of the method used and some indication of the relative size of each cohort, cannot be used to estimate the absolute size of the yearly birth cohorts. They are relative figures and therefore are affected by their neighbors; a cohort bounded by smaller sized cohorts appears larger than it actually should.

The second approximation trend line values, or the age heaping adjustment factors, were used to correct the enumerated populations.[17] In the 1900 census, the original age ratios as corrected by the final approximation of cohort size were used to adjust the enumerated populations. This procedure was followed because of the afore-mentioned deviation of 1900 from the trend in age heaping.

Special Adjustments for Age Heaping in Recent Censuses

When these age heaping adjustment factors were used, they resulted in an irregular pattern in the adjusted 1930, 1940, and 1950 figures at ages 10 and 20 for the native white females and at age 10 in 1930, 1940, and 1950 and age 30 in 1950 for the native white males. This irregularity seemed to be traceable to the original assumption of a linear trend in age heaping. It should be obvious that while a linear trend may be valid for a series of censuses it cannot continue indefinitely, for if such were the case all preferred ages would eventually become avoided and vice versa. In other words, if age heaping for age 40,

---

[17] Precisely speaking, the adjustments used a term which is a slight modification of the age ratio indicated by the trend line. If persons incorrectly reporting a given age typically have an age within five years of the one reported, an "age ratio" is not an appropriate divisor to remove the effect of age heaping. It will be shown that $CD = \dfrac{11AR}{10 + AR}$, where AR represents the age ratio and CD the true correction divisor. $AR = \dfrac{n + r}{n - \dfrac{r}{10}}$ (see footnote 5, this chapter), while $CD = \dfrac{n + r}{n}$ where n is the true number at the given age, and r the number falsely reporting the age. Then:

$$AR = \frac{n + r}{n} \times \frac{1}{1 - \dfrac{r}{10n}}$$

$$AR = CD \times \frac{1}{1 - \dfrac{r}{10n}}$$

$$AR = \frac{CD}{1 - \dfrac{CD}{10} + \dfrac{1}{10}}$$

$$10CD = 11AR - (CD)(AR)$$

$$CD = \frac{11AR}{10 + AR}$$

for example, has diminished in a linear fashion, a continuation of this trend would lead to age 40 becoming increasingly avoided, a highly doubtful conclusion.

The irregularity of the adjusted populations was manifested by peaks at the affected ages in the 1930, 1940, and 1950 censuses, the result of an over-correction for age heaping. In other words, the assumption of linearity in age heaping led to the improbable result of avoidance of young ages ending in 0. This irregularity alone could not be considered an adequate confirmation of incorrect adjustments for age heaping, however, as some of it could have been a reflection of true differences in the size of birth cohorts.

Additional empirical evidence supporting the argument against assuming continued linear trends of age heaping was provided by a comparison of the birth estimates (i.e., those derived from these adjusted populations) with those prepared by Whelpton from registered data. The three noticeable discrepancies in pattern occurred in 1919, 1929, and 1939,[18] with 1919 being the largest. These are exactly the three years in which such differences were to be expected (i.e., expected on the basis of the other two points) since those age 20 in 1940 and age 30 in 1950 provided the birth estimate for 1919, those age 20 in 1950 the birth estimate for 1929, and those age 10 in 1950 the birth estimate for 1939. The unmodified estimates of these three birth cohorts were not only larger than Whelpton's estimates but each was a peak where he showed a dip. The over-correction of the enumerated populations at these ages caused too large an estimation of births.

These three points all suggest that the trend of age heaping for the younger ages ending in 0 was less likely linear than leveling off and approaching unity asymptotically (or that the trend was curvilinear to some degree). It was assumed, therefore, that the age heaping adjustment factors for ages 10 and 20 in

[18] A test of the backward projection technique, described in the next chapter, was made by carrying the birth estimates as far forward as possible—to 1944. Even though the births from 1934 to 1944 were based on males from only one census the estimates showed a high degree of similarity with the registered births except for the noted differences; see Chapter 2, pages 14 and 16, and Figure 2, for a comparison of our estimates of the 1935–1944 births with adjusted registration figures.

1930, 1940, and 1950 for the females, and age 10 in 1930, 1940, and 1950 and age 30 in 1950 for the males, should not be allowed to go below unity and the enumerated populations at these ages were left unadjusted. If the trend of age heaping for these ages has in fact leveled off gradually, then the true correction factor should be slightly higher than 1.000. Making no adjustment at all at least prevents an over-correction of the enumerated population. The true correction factor is doubtless very close to unity.

This modified age adjustment eliminated the irregularity in the adjusted populations, and generated birth estimates which provided a much closer agreement with the pattern of Whelpton's estimates. The final adjustment factors, for both sexes, are shown in Tables 8 and 9. Figures 49 to 56 show the enumerated and adjusted native white female populations for the censuses of 1880 to 1950. The adjusted populations, while showing much smoother age distributions, retain genuine differences in cohort size.

TABLE 8

Age Heaping Correction Divisors, Native White Males, Ages 5–85, 1880–1950[a]

	Census							
Age	1880	1890	1900	1910	1920	1930	1940	1950
5	1.021	1.021	1.003	1.021	1.020	1.020	1.020	1.020
6	1.042	1.035	1.010	1.023	1.016	1.010	1.004	.997
7	.976	.981	.980	.990	.995	.999	1.004	1.008
8	1.009	1.009	1.003	1.009	1.008	1.008	1.008	1.008
9	.936	.948	1.003	.972	.984	.995	1.007	1.019
10	1.053	1.041	1.049	1.015	1.003	1.000[b]	1.000[b]	1.000[b]
11	.930	.937	.964	.950	.956	.963	.969	.975
12	1.080	1.073	1.007	1.059	1.052	1.044	1.037	1.030
13	.968	.972	.994	.979	.983	.986	.990	.994
14	1.040	1.036	.997	1.029	1.025	1.022	1.018	1.015
15	.931	.939	.974	.953	.961	.968	.975	.983
16	1.005	1.007	.999	1.013	1.015	1.018	1.021	1.024
17	.947	.958	.988	.980	.991	1.002	1.013	1.024
18	1.023	1.023	.991	1.023	1.022	1.022	1.022	1.022
19	.970	.974	.970	.984	.988	.993	.997	1.002
20	.962	.959	1.013	.953	.951	.948	.945	.942
21	1.058	1.051	1.033	1.036	1.029	1.022	1.015	1.007
22	1.034	1.027	1.025	1.013	1.005	.998	.991	.984
23	1.037	1.029	1.005	1.013	1.005	.996	.988	.980
24	1.011	1.010	1.010	1.008	1.007	1.006	1.005	1.005
25	1.000	.999	1.011	.997	.996	.995	.995	.994
26	.977	.980	.964	.985	.988	.991	.994	.996
27	.957	.964	.974	.976	.983	.989	.995	1.002
28	1.094	1.081	1.013	1.056	1.043	1.031	1.018	1.005
29	.873	.897	.957	.945	.969	.993	1.016	1.040
30	1.296	1.253	1.143	1.164	1.119	1.073	1.027	1.000[b]
31	.779	.803	.877	.850	.873	.896	.919	.942
32	.985	.990	.986	1.001	1.006	1.012	1.017	1.023
33	.926	.933	.959	.948	.955	.963	.970	.977
34	.908	.925	.967	.958	.974	.991	1.007	1.024
35	1.160	1.142	1.067	1.104	1.086	1.067	1.048	1.029
36	.947	.953	.967	.966	.973	.979	.985	.992
37	.880	.895	.953	.925	.940	.954	.969	.984
38	1.097	1.088	1.057	1.070	1.061	1.052	1.043	1.034
39	.927	.944	.994	.979	.996	1.014	1.031	1.048
40	1.345	1.303	1.159	1.219	1.176	1.133	1.089	1.045
41	.791	.807	.874	.839	.855	.871	.887	.903
42	1.003	1.015	.991	1.041	1.053	1.066	1.078	1.091
43	.878	.892	.928	.922	.937	.952	.966	.981
44	.887	.892	.959	.901	.905	.910	.915	.919
45	1.229	1.200	1.098	1.140	1.110	1.079	1.049	1.018
46	.905	.914	.929	.930	.939	.947	.955	.964
47	.881	.897	.957	.929	.944	.960	.975	.991
48	1.024	1.022	1.010	1.018	1.016	1.015	1.013	1.011
49	.897	.919	.975	.964	.985	1.007	1.029	1.051

(CONTINUED)

TABLE 8 (CONCLUDED)

				Census				
Age	1880	1890	1900	1910	1920	1930	1940	1950
50	1.372	1.332	1.214	1.252	1.211	1.170	1.128	1.087
51	.817	.828	.936	.851	.862	.873	.884	.895
52	1.076	1.075	1.043	1.073	1.072	1.071	1.070	1.070
53	.958	.962	.971	.969	.973	.976	.980	.984
54	.968	.973	.970	.982	.986	.991	.995	1.000
55	1.036	1.025	1.017	1.004	.993	.982	.971	.960
56	1.001	.995	.964	.985	.979	.974	.968	.963
57	.879	.889	.924	.907	.917	.926	.935	.944
58	.967	.972	.967	.981	.985	.990	.995	.999
59	.820	.851	.943	.910	.940	.969	.998	1.027
60	1.320	1.284	1.169	1.209	1.172	1.134	1.095	1.057
61	.787	.799	.879	.821	.833	.844	.855	.866
62	1.030	1.025	.999	1.016	1.012	1.007	1.003	.998
63	1.028	1.026	1.021	1.023	1.021	1.019	1.017	1.015
64	.950	.955	.985	.966	.972	.977	.983	.988
65	1.149	1.142	1.028	1.130	1.124	1.118	1.111	1.105
66	.918	.914	.951	.906	.903	.899	.895	.892
67	.892	.905	.992	.929	.941	.952	.964	.976
68	1.023	1.014	.979	.995	.986	.977	.968	.959
69	.878	.897	.941	.936	.955	.974	.994	1.013
70	1.197	1.172	1.096	1.123	1.098	1.073	1.048	1.023
71	.782	.800	.891	.836	.853	.871	.889	.906
72	1.015	1.017	1.001	1.023	1.025	1.028	1.031	1.034
73	.957	.962	.976	.971	.975	.980	.985	.989
74	.963	.965	.971	.971	.974	.976	.979	.982
75	1.033	1.032	1.018	1.030	1.029	1.028	1.027	1.026
76	.962	.959	.933	.953	.951	.948	.945	.942
77	.864	.873	.987	.892	.901	.910	.919	.929
78	1.042	1.029	1.003	1.004	.991	.978	.965	.952
79	.858	.879	.909	.922	.943	.964	.985	1.006
80	1.142	1.119	1.008	1.075	1.052	1.030	1.007	.985
81	.808	.822	.913	.851	.865	.879	.892	.906
82	.974	.974	.958	.972	.971	.970	.969	.968
83	.942	.951	.940	.967	.975	.984	.992	1.000
84	1.024	1.021	.976	1.015	1.013	1.010	1.007	1.005
85	.925	.924	.918	.922	.921	.920	.919	.918

[a] These figures were used to correct the census enumerated populations for age heaping. The figures for 1880, 1890, and 1910–1950 represent the adjusted final trend lines, the derivation of which is described in footnote 17, p. 124. The figures for 1900 are the life table adjusted age ratios corrected for cohort size.

[b] These age ratios have not been allowed to go below unit by assumption; see pp. 125–126.

TABLE 9
Age Heaping Correction Divisors, Native White Females, Ages 5–85,
1880–1950[a]

	Census							
Age	1880	1890	1900	1910	1920	1930	1940	1950
5	1.027	1.025	1.001	1.022	1.020	1.018	1.016	1.015
6	1.055	1.046	1.007	1.028	1.019	1.010	1.001	.992
7	.980	.985	.984	.994	.998	1.003	1.007	1.012
8	1.021	1.019	1.010	1.015	1.014	1.012	1.010	1.008
9	.934	.945	.998	.967	.978	.989	1.000	1.011
10	1.033	1.024	1.044	1.008	1.000	1.000[b]	1.000[b]	1.000[b]
11	.930	.938	.964	.954	.963	.971	.979	.987
12	1.062	1.056	.998	1.043	1.037	1.031	1.024	1.018
13	.960	.965	.984	.976	.982	.987	.993	.998
14	1.007	1.007	.988	1.007	1.008	1.008	1.008	1.008
15	.931	.939	.972	.953	.961	.968	.975	.983
16	1.034	1.030	1.004	1.023	1.019	1.015	1.012	1.008
17	.945	.953	.991	.970	.978	.986	.995	1.003
18	1.097	1.086	1.015	1.062	1.051	1.039	1.027	1.015
19	.948	.956	.986	.973	.981	.989	.997	1.005
20	1.090	1.070	1.051	1.031	1.011	1.000[b]	1.000[b]	1.000[b]
21	.927	.939	.973	.963	.974	.986	.998	1.010
22	1.060	1.050	1.030	1.030	1.020	1.010	1.000	.990
23	1.011	1.009	1.009	1.005	1.004	1.002	1.000	.998
24	1.020	1.018	1.016	1.015	1.013	1.011	1.009	1.007
25	1.046	1.043	1.031	1.035	1.032	1.028	1.024	1.021
26	.985	.987	.973	.991	.993	.995	.996	.998
27	.918	.928	.970	.946	.955	.964	.974	.983
28	1.087	1.076	1.005	1.054	1.043	1.033	1.022	1.011
29	.828	.856	.940	.912	.940	.967	.995	1.022
30	1.295	1.258	1.127	1.183	1.145	1.107	1.069	1.030
31	.747	.774	.879	.827	.853	.879	.905	.931
32	1.009	1.014	.995	1.023	1.027	1.032	1.036	1.041
33	.917	.924	.962	.939	.946	.953	.961	.968
34	.905	.918	.972	.944	.957	.970	.983	.995
35	1.138	1.124	1.052	1.095	1.081	1.067	1.052	1.038
36	.985	.985	.975	.985	.984	.984	.984	.984
37	.892	.901	.954	.918	.926	.934	.942	.951
38	1.105	1.099	1.048	1.087	1.080	1.074	1.068	1.061
39	.891	.912	.992	.954	.975	.996	1.017	1.038
40	1.370	1.331	1.151	1.250	1.209	1.168	1.127	1.085
41	.752	.769	.867	.803	.820	.837	.854	.871
42	1.012	1.024	.998	1.047	1.059	1.070	1.082	1.094
43	.893	.905	.947	.927	.938	.949	.960	.971
44	.921	.921	.970	.921	.921	.921	.921	.921
45	1.205	1.179	1.070	1.128	1.103	1.077	1.051	1.024
46	.899	.904	.934	.913	.918	.922	.927	.931
47	.879	.892	.969	.916	.928	.940	.952	.964
48	1.061	1.058	1.027	1.052	1.050	1.047	1.044	1.042
49	.883	.905	.980	.950	.972	.994	1.015	1.037

(CONTINUED)

TABLE 9 (CONCLUDED)

				Census				
Age	1880	1890	1900	1910	1920	1930	1940	1950
50	1.436	1.395	1.213	1.310	1.267	1.224	1.180	1.136
51	.769	.785	.906	.815	.830	.845	.860	.875
52	1.024	1.029	1.000	1.038	1.043	1.047	1.052	1.056
53	.902	.911	.941	.930	.939	.948	.957	.966
54	.997	.997	.978	.997	.996	.996	.996	.996
55	1.056	1.045	1.037	1.024	1.013	1.002	.991	.980
56	1.014	1.004	.982	.984	.974	.964	.953	.943
57	.852	.865	.934	.892	.905	.918	.930	.943
58	.994	.999	.978	1.010	1.015	1.021	1.026	1.032
59	.819	.848	.950	.905	.934	.963	.991	1.019
60	1.416	1.372	1.206	1.282	1.236	1.190	1.143	1.096
61	.742	.758	.863	.790	.806	.822	.838	.854
62	.995	.994	.977	.990	.988	.986	.985	.983
63	.989	.990	.999	.992	.993	.994	.995	.995
64	.961	.962	.983	.964	.964	.965	.966	.967
65	1.193	1.185	1.057	1.169	1.161	1.153	1.145	1.137
66	.916	.914	.960	.910	.908	.906	.905	.903
67	.890	.899	.965	.918	.927	.936	.945	.954
68	1.021	1.017	.975	1.010	1.006	1.003	.999	.995
69	.833	.858	.941	.908	.933	.958	.983	1.007
70	1.267	1.240	1.133	1.186	1.159	1.132	1.104	1.077
71	.722	.744	.860	.787	.809	.831	.852	.874
72	.995	.998	.989	1.004	1.006	1.009	1.012	1.015
73	.939	.943	.940	.952	.957	.962	.966	.971
74	.959	.958	.968	.956	.955	.954	.953	.952
75	1.095	1.090	1.055	1.081	1.077	1.072	1.068	1.063
76	.978	.974	.945	.964	.960	.955	.951	.946
77	.877	.881	.964	.891	.895	.900	.905	.909
78	1.024	1.014	.974	.994	.984	.974	.964	.953
79	.819	.842	.892	.889	.912	.935	.958	.981
80	1.165	1.148	1.054	1.114	1.097	1.080	1.063	1.046
81	.760	.778	.885	.814	.832	.850	.867	.885
82	.954	.958	.945	.965	.969	.973	.976	.980
83	.954	.960	.945	.971	.976	.982	.987	.993
84	1.082	1.068	.986	1.039	1.024	1.010	.995	.981
85	.982	.976	.941	.965	.960	.954	.949	.943

[a] These figures were used to correct the census enumerated populations for age heaping. The figures for 1880, 1890, and 1910–1950 represent the adjusted final trend lines, the derivation of which is described in footnote 17, p. 124. The figures for 1900 are the life table adjusted age ratios corrected for cohort size.

[b] These age ratios have not been allowed to go below unity by assumption; see p. 126.

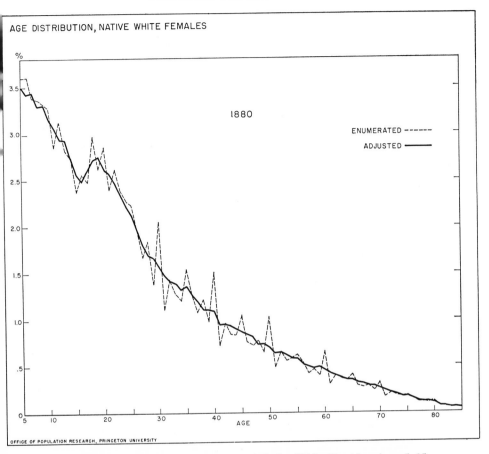

FIGURE 49.   Per Cent Distribution of Native White Females, Ages 5–85,
as Enumerated by the Census and as Adjusted for Age Heaping: 1880.
Source: See footnote 6, Chapter 7 and relevant citations in Appendix A for sources
of enumerated population

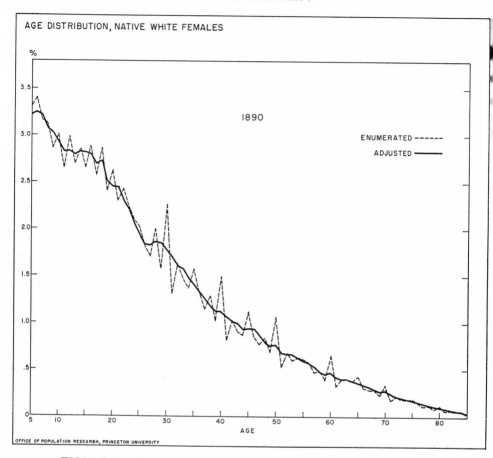

FIGURE 50. Per Cent Distribution of Native White Females, Ages 5–85, as Enumerated by the Census and as Adjusted for Age Heaping: 1890.
Source: See footnote 6, Chapter 7 and relevant citations in Appendix A for sources of enumerated population

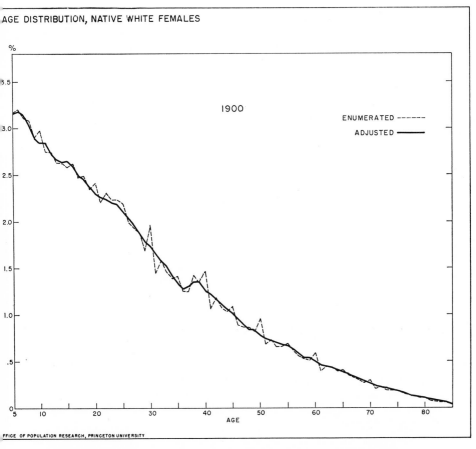

AGE DISTRIBUTION, NATIVE WHITE FEMALES

FIGURE 51.   Per Cent Distribution of Native White Females, Ages 5–85,
as Enumerated by the Census and as Adjusted for Age Heaping: 1900.
Source: See footnote 6, Chapter 7 and relevant citations in Appendix A for sources
of enumerated population

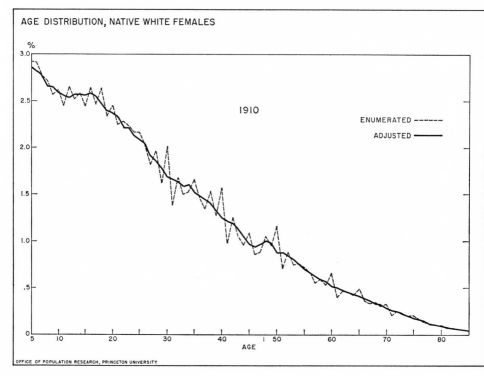

FIGURE 52.   Per Cent Distribution of Native White Females, Ages 5–85,
as Enumerated by the Census and as Adjusted for Age Heaping: 1910.
Source: See footnote 6, Chapter 7 and relevant citations in Appendix A for sources
of enumerated population

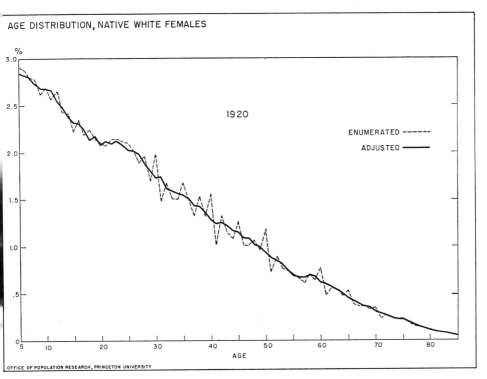

FIGURE 53. Per Cent Distribution of Native White Females, Ages 5–85, as Enumerated by the Census and as Adjusted for Age Heaping: 1920.
Source: See footnote 6, Chapter 7 and relevant citations in Appendix A for sources of enumerated population

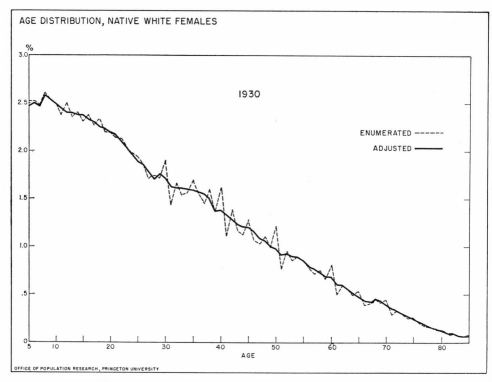

FIGURE 54.   Per Cent Distribution of Native White Females, Ages 5–85,
as Enumerated by the Census and as Adjusted for Age Heaping: 1930.
Source: See footnote 6, Chapter 7 and relevant citations in Appendix A for sources
of enumerated population

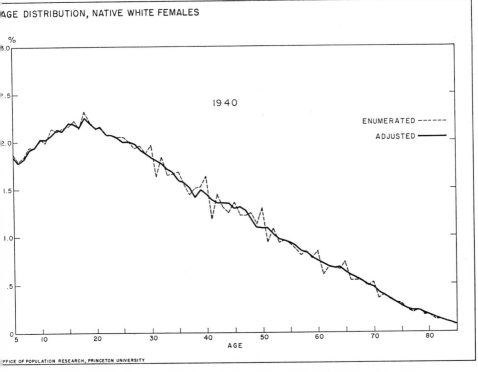

AGE DISTRIBUTION, NATIVE WHITE FEMALES

1940

ENUMERATED - - - - -
ADJUSTED ———

OFFICE OF POPULATION RESEARCH, PRINCETON UNIVERSITY

FIGURE 55.   Per Cent Distribution of Native White Females, Ages 5–85,
as Enumerated by the Census and as Adjusted for Age Heaping: 1940.
Source: See footnote 6, Chapter 7 and relevant citations in Appendix A for sources
of enumerated population

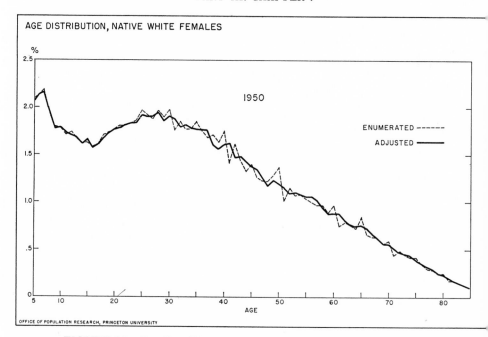

FIGURE 56.   Per Cent Distribution of Native White Females, Ages 5–85,
as Enumerated by the Census and as Adjusted for Age Heaping: 1950.
Source: See footnote 6, Chapter 7 and relevant citations in Appendix A for sources
of enumerated population

Chapter 8. Estimating Annual Births and Birth Rates

Chapter 2 has already presented a simplified description of the manner in which the birth estimates were prepared from the age-heaping adjusted populations. In this chapter we are primarily concerned with pointing out the technical problems and possible sources of error encountered in the course of preparing these estimates.

The appropriate equation for estimating births[1] in 1905 from the 1950 census age distribution, for example, would be:

$$(1) \quad B_{1905} = ({}_1P_{44})_{1950} \times \left(\frac{{}_1L_{34}}{{}_1L_{44}}\right)_{1940-1950} \times \left(\frac{{}_1L_{24}}{{}_1L_{34}}\right)_{1930-1940}$$
$$\times \left(\frac{{}_1L_{14}}{{}_1L_{24}}\right)_{1920-1930} \times \left(\frac{{}_1L_{4}}{{}_1L_{14}}\right)_{1910-1920} \times \left(\frac{{}_1{}_0}{{}_1L_{4}}\right)_{1900-1910}$$

where B_{1905} equals births in the year 1905, $({}_1P_{44})_{1950}$ equals the population age 44 in 1950, and the other factors represent decade life table inverse survivorship ratios.[2]

Conversion to Calendar-Year Estimates

Equation (1) ignores the fact that births estimated from the various censuses represent "census-year" births rather than calendar-year births. For example, births estimated from the 1950 census by the use of Eq. (1) would be for twelve-month periods beginning April 1. Since the several censuses provide estimates covering different twelve-month periods, it is necessary to make a conversion, at some point in the computations, to estimates for comparable time periods. We have adjusted our estimates to January 1–December 31 periods, thereby conforming to standard practice.

This conversion could have been made after the "census-

---

[1] The techniques for projecting backwards to birth were the same for both sexes (or the same in so far as circumstances would allow; see below, pp. 142–143). The methods by which the several observations for each year were combined differed, however. The differences, and the reasons underlying them, are explained in subsequent sections of this chapter.

[2] The various decade life tables used do not always cover equal periods of time. Thus the life table used for the 1920's is the 1920–1929 life table, while the one used between 1940 and 1950 can be considered to represent the period 1940–1950. See Appendix B for the methods used in constructing and adjusting the decade life tables.

year" births were computed, by taking weighted averages of two adjacent "census-year" estimates. With estimates derived from the 1950 census, for example, three-fourths of one year's figure plus one-fourth of the figure for the previous year would give the number of births from January 1 to December 31.

Instead of converting from "census-year" births, we have projected the populations back to age 1, converted to calendar-year estimates, and then carried this estimate back to birth by allowing for infant mortality. This procedure was followed because of the relatively large annual variability at age 0 of the probability of dying. Conversion of the census-based estimates of the population age 1 to calendar-year estimates was accomplished by weighting two successive estimates, the weights used depending on the day the census was taken.

Adjusting for Infant Mortality

Aside from the errors inherent in the construction and adjustment of the life tables and the "smoothing" effects resulting from converting to calendar-years, Eq. (1) involves certain other errors, especially when a birth cohort has not lived through a complete decade. The 1900–1910 life table gives the average mortality experience of those who lived through the entire decade. The birth cohort of 1905, however, lived through only the last six years of the decade. As a result the inverse survivorship ratio from this life table is too high, because of the decline in mortality that occurred during the decade. The consequence is an estimate of births which is too high. The error introduced here is probably quite small, especially in view of the correction factor introduced for infant mortality, where the highest percentage increase in survivorship occurred.

Although infant mortality has generally been decreasing in this country there have, of course, been yearly fluctuations about the trend. The use of decade life tables not only ignores the trend, over a ten-year range, but also ignores the annual fluctuations about the trend. It therefore seemed essential to devise corrected $_1q_0$'s which would reflect, on an annual basis, the downward trend in infant mortality and its annual fluctuations.

The first step in preparing these adjusted $_1q_0$'s was to interpolate between the $_1q_0$'s given in life tables centered on the end years of each decade. Annual fluctuations were then introduced by assuming that the yearly fluctuations in the 0–1 death rate (i.e., $_1m_0$) about a ten-year trend line were representative of the yearly fluctuations in the $_1q_0$ values. For example, the 1939, 1940, and 1941 values of $_1m_0$ were averaged and centered on 1940 while the 1949, 1950, and 1951 values were averaged and centered on 1950. Expected values for each year in between these points were determined by linear interpolation. The ratio of this expected $_1m_0$ to the actual $_1m_0$ for each year was calculated and applied to the expected $_1q_0$ calculated by linear interpolation between the $_1q_0$'s given for the 1940 and 1950 Life Tables. This gave an "actual" $_1q_0$ corrected for yearly fluctuations in the $_1m_0$ rate.

There was no way of adjusting for the annual fluctuations in infant mortality prior to 1901 because of the unavailability of data. Cognizance was taken however of the general downward trend in infant mortality by interpolating between the $_1q_0$ values from each decade life table to obtain a separate value for each year.

ADJUSTING FOR THE 1918 INFLUENZA EPIDEMIC

Another adjustment was introduced to account for the effect of the 1918 influenza epidemic. Since a life table covering the period 1910–1920 was derived by taking an average of appropriate values from the 1909–1911 and 1919–1921 life tables, it does not reflect the sharp increase in mortality that occurred in 1918 as a result of the epidemic. Survivors projected backward on the basis of this life table would therefore give too few births.

This correction for the increase in mortality in 1918 was based on the assumption that the increase in the death rate $(_1m_x)$ for that year, over the "expected" value determined by linear interpolation between the 1910 and 1920 values, was representative of the increase in the $_1q_x$ value.

The 1909, 1910, and 1911 values of $_nm_x$ for each age group were averaged and centered on 1910 while the 1919, 1920, and 1921 values for each age group were averaged and centered on 1920. By simple interpolation between these points, an expected value for 1918 was calculated. The ratio of the actual value to the expected was taken for each age-group; these ratios were centered on the mid-point of each age group. Intermediate values for each single year of age were then estimated by interpolating between these values, giving a yearly ratio of the actual $_1m_x$ to the expected $_1m_x$.

The expected values of the $_1q_x$'s for 1918 were arrived at by interpolating between the 1910 and 1920 values of $_1q_x$. The ratios of the actual to the expected $_1m_x$'s were then applied to the expected $_1q_x$'s to provide corrected "actual" $_1q_x$ values.

Equation (1) with these various refinements thus becomes:

$$(2) \quad B_{1905} = (_1P_{44})_{1950} \times \left(\frac{_1L_{34}}{_1L_{44}}\right)_{1940-1950} \times \left(\frac{_1L_{24}}{_1L_{34}}\right)_{1930-1940}$$
$$\times \left(\frac{_1L_{14}}{_1L_{24}}\right)_{1920-1930} \times \left(\frac{_1L_{4}}{_1L_{14}}\right)_{1910-1920} \times \left(\frac{_1l_{1}}{_1L_{4}}\right)_{1900-1910}$$
$$\times \frac{p_{13}}{p'_{13}} \times \left(\frac{1}{_1p_0}\right)_{1905}$$

where p_{13} is the estimated normal probability of surviving from age 13 to 14 in 1918 and p'_{13} is the estimated probability with the excess mortality caused by the influenza epidemic: $\left(\frac{1}{_1p_0}\right)_{1905}$ is the inverse survivorship ratio for births occurring in 1905; all other factors are the same as previously mentioned; and where the first two factors are applied after the conversion to calendar-year periods.

ADJUSTING THE MALES FOR WAR LOSSES

The 1910–1920 and 1940–1950 life tables were constructed from other life tables and do not reflect the increased male mortality resulting from military service in World War I and World War II. It was necessary, therefore, to devise a correction similar to that for influenza to account for the excess male mortality. For each war the excess mortality (i.e., the difference between total male deaths, including those caused by the war, and the deaths that would have occurred had there been no war) was calculated and used in conjunction with expected $_1m_x$ values to adjust expected $_1q_x$ values.

All estimated military deaths were assigned to one calendar-year in each war—1918 and 1944. A total $_nm_x$ for each age group was calculated by adding to the civilian $_nm_x$ (e.g., in 1944) the $_nm_x$ reflecting the excess mortality to each age-group resulting from the war. These corrected (i.e., total) $_nm_x$ values were centered on the midyear of each age group, intermediate values being determined by linear interpolation. Expected $_nm_x$ values for 1944 were determined by averaging the 1939, 1940, and 1941 $_nm_x$ values and the 1949, 1950, and 1951 $_nm_x$ values and interpolating between the two averages; by centering the expected $_nm_x$ for each age-group in the central age, and interpolating, values for each year of age were obtained.[3] The ratio of the expected $_1m_x$ to the actual $_1m_x$ provided a correction factor which was applied to the actual $_1q_x$ in order to obtain an expected $_1q_x$. These expected $_1q_x$'s reflected the mortality experience of civilian males and military personnel.

ESTIMATING BIRTHS FROM THE 1890 CENSUS

A slightly different formula was required in estimating births from the population enumerated in the 1890 census. Because of the difference in this census of the question relating to age, the average age of the group enumerated at any age x is not $x + .5$ (as in the other censuses) but exact age x. Consequently, the inverse survivorship ratios used to project these people backwards was calculated from the l_x columns of the life tables rather than from the $_1L_x$ columns. For example, the birth cohort of 1881, as estimated from the 1890 census, was calculated from the product of $(_1P_9)_{1890}$, $\left(\dfrac{l_1}{l_9}\right)_{1880-1890}$ and $\left(\dfrac{1}{_1p_0}\right)_{1881}$.

---

[3] This form of estimation—assigning the mean value for an age interval to the central age, and obtaining single-year values by interpolation—maintains the original grouped data unchanged only when the function being interpolated is linear. The assumption of linearity creates consequential departures from the original data when the grouped mortality rate is a maximum. (The same problem would also be associated with minima.) The given form of estimation would assign this maximum value only to the mid-point of the interval, and would assign lower values to all other points. It is obvious that the average of the interpolated single-year values for the interval would be less than the observed average here ascribed to the mid-point. We have assigned a value to the mid-point that preserves the observed average for the interval. This assigned value is

$$\frac{8y_m - y_{m-1} - y_{m+1}}{6}$$

where m is the interval in which the grouped data reach the maximum, $m - 1$ and $m + 1$ are the preceding and succeeding intervals, and the y's are grouped rates.

Combining the Female Estimates

On the basis of evidence already cited concerning the consistency of birth estimates from females of different ages in the several censuses,[4] a single series of annual female births was constructed from the estimates derived from females aged 15 to 29 in each census. The births estimated from each census were overlapped for five years at either end and provided figures independently for five years.[5] The overlapping figures were combined by weighting the two observations with the weights gradually increasing for the later census. This procedure was followed to reduce spurious fluctuations in going from one census to the next.

Combining the Male Estimates

Unlike the females, the males did not show a tendency to be better enumerated at some ages than at others. In other words, births calculated from males at the young ages in one census tended to be approximately equal to those calculated from a later enumeration of the same cohort, at least up to age 55 or 60.

The exceptions to consistent estimates are those based on the 1890 and 1920 censuses. The former census provided estimates which were at the same general level as the estimates from other censuses but there were several instances of sharp differences in pattern between the births from the 1890 census and the births from other censuses.[6] On the other hand, births calculated from the 1920 census tended generally to be below those from adjacent censuses especially among the males.[7] It was therefore decided

---

[4] See Chapter 2, pp. 10–11.

[5] The 1880 and 1890 censuses overlap for four years while the 1890 and 1900 censuses overlap for six years, a result of the difference in the age question of the 1890 census.

[6] This condition was not as serious with the females, mainly as a result of the restriction, with them, to the use of birth estimates derived from the 15- to 29-year-olds only.

[7] This may have resulted in small part from the population overseas in 1920. There was a total of 152,000 persons abroad in 1920 for whom no age, sex, nativity classification was provided. It is likely that native white males between the ages of 17 and 35 comprised the major share of these persons. However, no attempt was made to apportion these people or to include them in the distributions used to estimate births.

144

to eliminate the 1890 and 1920 censuses (or the birth estimates derived from them) in producing the single annual series of male births.

FINAL ADJUSTMENT TO THE 1917–1934 ESTIMATES

One final adjustment was made to a portion of the birth series. The births from 1917 to 1934 were adjusted to reflect the information at our disposal about annual variations in births in these years from the birth register. The necessity for this adjustment came to our attention when we noticed discrepancies between our estimates and those prepared by P. K. Whelpton, who adjusted registered births (beginning in 1909) for incomplete national coverage and under-registration.[8] We were not disturbed by the difference in the *level* of Whelpton's estimates and ours, since his adjustments are acknowledged to be especially conjectural for the earlier years (Figure 57). However, it did seem likely that year-to-year variations were more accurately represented by registered data than by estimates based on the backward projection of census counts adjusted for age heaping. One reason for preferring the variations indicated by registered data is that the census-based birth estimates during this span of years were April to April births, and the estimation of calendar-year variations from April to April data would necessarily be blurred, even if the latter were perfectly accurate.

The assumption upon which the adjustment was based is that our estimates provided an acceptable indication of the level of births (as reflected in a moving average), and that registered data provided the best indication of annual variations (as reflected in deviations from a moving average).

Five-year moving averages were computed from the registered births for the period 1915 to 1936. In computing these averages, however, it was necessary to avoid including a state as soon as it entered the Birth Registration Area. Immediate inclusion of a new state would result in spurious increases in the averages and consequently in the annual variations. At the same time, restriction of the states used to the original area would mean

---

[8] U.S. National Office of Vital Statistics, "Births and Birth Rates in the Entire United States 1909–1948," prepared by P. K. Whelpton, *Vital Statistics—Special Reports*, Vol. 33, No. 8 (1950).

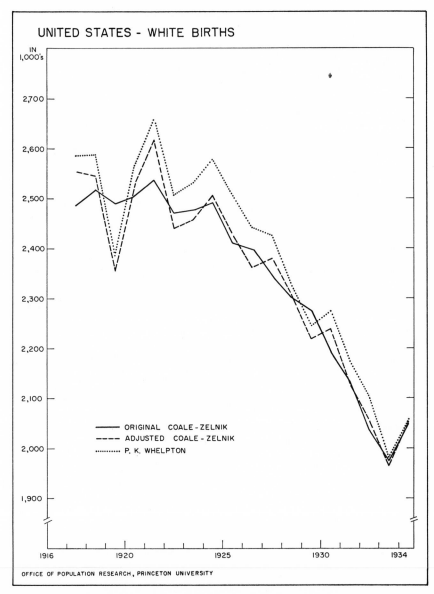

FIGURE 57. United States White Births, 1917–1934—
Estimates of Whelpton and Coale-Zelnik.

not using all of the available data, and possibly decreasing the representativeness of the sample.

This problem was solved by including additional states in the computation after they had been in the Birth Registration Area for five years. In the few instances where a state was dropped from the Birth Registration Area, it also was not included in the calculations for the period two years prior to when it was dropped. For example, Nebraska entered the Birth Registration Area in 1920; it was not included in the computations until computing the average centered on 1922, when there were five years of data available for the state. South Carolina entered the Birth Registration Area in 1919, was dropped in 1925, and re-entered in 1928. Its data was used in computing averages centered on 1921 and 1922 and not again until computing the average centered on 1930.

The ratio of the annual number of births (for the states used in computing the average) to the five-year moving average centered on that year was then computed. This ratio was then applied to a five-year moving average calculated from the estimated births.[9]

[9] In computing the five-year moving average centered on 1934, it was necessary to have births for 1935 and 1936. These were computed from the males aged (approximately) 14 and 13 in 1950; these estimates were then increased by 3.0 per cent, the upward adjustment factor cited in Chapter 2. Births for these two years were then arrived at in the same way as births for the earlier years and gave a more consistent average than would have been the case if total registered births for 1935 and 1936 had been used.

Chapter 9. Estimating Census Enumeration Errors

The series of annual white births shown in Table 1, Chapter 3, and estimated by the techniques described in Chapters 2 and 8, are calendar-year births, i.e., they relate to January 1–December 31 periods. As such, these births cannot be used to estimate the expected population at each age in any census except that of 1920, since all other censuses were taken as of some day other than January 1. Using calendar-year births to estimate enumeration errors in these other censuses would mean that we were not relating the enumerated populations to the actual births of which they were the survivors and would thereby be introducing a source of error. For example, persons correctly enumerated at age 6 in the 1930 census were born between April 1, 1923 and March 31, 1924; conversely, of the persons born between January 1 and December 31, 1923, three-fourths were age 6 at the time of the 1930 census, and one-fourth were age 7. If the number of births occurring between January 1–March 31, 1923 and January 1–March 31, 1924 differed, use of the 1923 calendar-year births would produce an erroneous estimate of the number of 6 year olds expected in the 1930 census, and consequently, an erroneous estimate of the enumeration error at this age.

The differences in the days on which the censuses were taken (also the difference in the 1890 census in the question pertaining to age) meant that it was necessary to prepare several series of annual births, in addition to the January 1–December 31 series (which was used to estimate the expected populations in the 1920 census). One series covered births occurring from June 1 to May 31 of the following year and was used in conjunction with the 1880 and 1900 census; another series provided April 1–March 31 births and was used to estimate the errors in the 1910, 1930, 1940, and 1950 censuses;[1] the final series was for use in estimating the expected 1890 populations.[2]

---

[1] The 1910 census was taken as of April 15; the 14-day difference was taken into account in estimating the calendar-year births but has here been ignored.

[2] Although the 1890 census was taken as of June 1, the different age question required that it be treated separately, and differently, from the 1880 and 1900 censuses.

Each series was prepared in essentially the same manner: the populations at the selected ages in each census (i.e., 15–29 for the females, and 5–59 for the males) were projected back to birth; estimates for a twelve-month period other than the one being prepared were converted to the proper time-base by interpolating between the birth estimates for two successive years.[3] For example, in preparing the April 1–March 31 birth series, the populations of all censuses were first projected back to birth. No adjustment was necessary with the estimates derived from the 1910, 1930, 1940, and 1950 censuses. To convert the June 1–May 31 births estimated from the 1880 and 1900 censuses to April 1–March 31 births, five-sixths of one year's estimate was added to one-sixth of the previous year's estimate. In a similar way, i.e., by the proper weighting, births derived from the 1920 and 1890 censuses were also converted to April 1–March 31 births.

After the estimates derived from all censuses represented the same twelve-month periods, construction of the birth series proceeded in the same way as the January 1–December 31 series; i.e., births derived from the females aged 15 to 29 (approximately) were combined by overlapping the estimates from the several censuses, births derived from males aged 5 to 59 (approximately) were combined by averaging the estimates from the usable censuses (here again, the estimates based on the 1890 and 1920 censuses were not used), with the latter series being increased by the overall percentage difference between it and the series based on females. The upward adjusted estimates based on the males and the estimates derived from the females were then averaged to produce the required series.

ADJUSTMENT OF THE APRIL 1–MARCH 31 BIRTH SERIES

An adjustment similar to the one described in the previous chapter was applied to the April–March birth series to take account of the annual variations in the registered births in all years from 1917 on. Although registered births are given by month of occurrence for total births, no color breakdown is provided (at least not until 1942) so that the adjustment introduced here was

---

[3] In this respect these additional birth series differed from the January 1–December 31 series, where the projection back to birth followed the conversion to the proper time period (i.e., calendar-year periods).

somewhat indirect compared to the one applied to the January–December series.

The first step was to compute, for a constant number of states, five-year moving averages of April–March total registered births and then calculate the ratio of the annual April–March total registered births (for the same states) to the average. The same computation was then made for January–December total registered births (again for the same states), i.e., the ratio of annual births to a five-year moving average. The ratio of these two ratios, reflecting the difference between the annual variation of April–March total births (for 10 states) from a five-year moving average and the annual variation of January–December total births (for 10 states) from a comparable five-year moving average was assumed to equal the difference between the annual variation of April–March white births (for the United States) from a five-year moving average of such births and the annual variation of January–December white births (for the United States) from its five-year moving average. Since it was not possible to compute the latter ratio, use was made of the ratios calculated for the adjustment in the previous chapter, i.e., an increasing number of states. The entire computational scheme is shown in Eq. (1), below, where:

$$(a) = \frac{\text{April–March total births, 10 states}}{\text{Five-year moving average April–March total births, 10 states}}$$

$$(b) = \frac{\text{January–December total births, 10 states}}{\text{Five-year moving average January–December total births, 10 states}}$$

$$(c) = \frac{\text{April–March white births, United States}}{\text{Five-year moving average April–March white births, United States}}$$

$$(d) = \frac{\text{January–December white births, 10 or more states}}{\text{Five-year moving average January–December white births, 10 or more states}}$$

and where the April–March white births for the United States [i.e., the numerator of (c)] are the figures being estimated.

(1) $$\frac{(a)}{(b)} = \frac{(c)}{(d)}$$

Estimating the Expected Census Populations

Births of each series were then projected forward, separately by sex, to estimate the number of native white persons expected at each age in the appropriate census.[4] This forward projecting is simply the reverse of the backward projecting technique and utilizes, with two exceptions, the same life table ratios. The two exceptions occurred in estimating the expected populations age 0 and 1 in the 1890 census. The population age 0 at the time of the 1890 census were those infants born in the previous six months. (The question "age at nearest birthday" meant those born 7 to 12 months prior to the census should have been enumerated at age 1.) It was therefore necessary to have a life table function which gave the number of people alive from time of birth to age 6 months, rather than the number of people alive between time of birth and 1 year of age. In short, it was necessary to use $_{1/2}L_0$ in the forward projection rather than $_1L_0$. The population age 0 could then be estimated from the product of B_{1890} and $\left(\dfrac{_{1/2}L_0}{1_0}\right)_{1880-1890}$, where B_{1890} equals the number of births estimated for the six-month period prior to June 1, 1890, and $\left(\dfrac{_{1/2}L_0}{1_0}\right)_{1880-1890}$ the life table survivorship ratio for the first six months of life.

While our 1880–1890 life table did not provide $_{1/2}L_0$, it was possible to approximate it by using, as a correction factor, the ratio of $\dfrac{_{1/2}L_0}{_1L_0}$ from a life table (of assumed similar mortality conditions) where $_{1/2}L_0$ was available. This ratio, obtained from the 1901 life tables for native whites,[5] was multiplied against the $(_1L_0)_{1880-1890}$ to provide $(_{1/2}L_0)_{1880-1890}$.

The population age 1 in the 1890 census were those births which had occurred six to eighteen months prior to the census; i.e., children who had lived six full months or more but less than eighteen months. Although the probability of survival is higher in the second six months of life than in the first six months, it is

---

[4] Appendix A contains a discussion of the effects of the differences in the reported census age-distributions for native whites on the estimates of births and under-enumeration.

[5] Glover, *op. cit.*, Tables 19 and 21.

still appreciably below the probability of surviving the immediate subsequent six-month periods. Estimating the number at age 1 meant that we would have to take into account the probability of surviving this second six months of life plus the higher probability of surviving the following six-month period. In this instance therefore it was necessary to have an approximation to $_1L_{1/2}$. This approximation worked out to be equal to

$$\left[({_1L_0} - {_{1/2}L_0}) + \frac{3l_1 + l_2}{8} \right].$$

A similar procedure could have been followed for the populations expected at all other ages in the 1890 census. However, since the risk of mortality and the change in this risk from one age to the next are greatest in the first twelve months of life (ignoring the old ages, which in this instance are not involved), it was felt that the possible gain in accuracy was very slight and would not warrant the effort. Ages beyond 1 therefore have not been subjected to this refinement.

Estimating the Population 0–4 in the 1940 Census and the Population 0–14 in the 1950 Census

The expected populations 0–4 in 1940 and 0–14 in 1950 were estimated from registered births adjusted for under-registration. It was first necessary to obtain registered white births for twelve-month periods beginning April 1. For the cohorts born April 1942–March 1943 and after, these figures were immediately available from official sources. For the cohorts born April 1935–March 1936 to April 1941–March 1942, an adjustment was made to the registered calendar-year births since monthly births during this interval are not given by color. It was assumed that the ratio of interpolated white male births (i.e., three-fourths the births of one year plus one-fourth the births of the following year) to interpolated total births was equal to the ratio of registered white male births April–March to total registered births April–March.

After converting to April–March births, it was necessary to adjust all of these cohorts for under-registration. The official estimates of under-registration were not used as given since these estimates apply to calendar-year births. Instead, we assumed equality between the ratio of adjusted (for under-registration) interpolated births to registered interpolated births and the ratio of adjusted April–March births to the (estimated) registered April–March births.

These April–March births, adjusted for under-registration, were then projected forward to estimate the expected populations. While the technique used was the same as with other birth cohorts, one further adjustment was introduced. Instead of using a calendar-year probability of survival for age 0, an interpolated value was used, estimated by taking three-fourths the value of one year plus one-fourth the value of the following year.

Estimating the Expected 1960 White Population

The availability of annual white births makes it possible to estimate the native white populations expected at each age in the 1960 census. It is not possible, though, to estimate the errors in the enumeration of these populations since tabulations of the enumerated native whites, by age and sex, are not yet available. The Bureau of the Census, however, has completed tabulating the counts of total whites, by age and sex, for the United States. We have therefore, prepared preliminary and approximate estimates of the enumeration errors in the counts of total whites, by age and sex, for the area defined as conterminous United States.

The Bureau of the Census periodically prepares estimates of the population by age, color, and sex. These estimates are based on the last census and the net changes to the various groups through births, deaths, and net migration. These components of change are independent of the census enumeration and of the enumeration errors. By taking the net changes over the ten-year interval April 1, 1950–1960, and adding them to our estimated 1950 census populations, we can estimate the expected 1960 counts and consequently the errors in this census.

A number of adjustments and corrections had to be made before we could estimate the net changes between April 1, 1950 and April 1, 1960. No estimate was prepared by the Bureau of the Census for April 1, 1960; there are, however, estimates for July 1, 1958 and July 1, 1959. We used these two estimates to prepare, by extrapolation, an estimate for April 1, 1960. In the case of the July 1, 1959 estimate, we first had to subtract the population of Alaska; this was done by assuming that the estimated July 1, 1959 population of Alaska had the same age, color, sex distribution as the enumerated April 1, 1960 Alaska population. After calculating the extrapolated April 1, 1960 estimates, we subtracted the 1950 census counts; the differences represented the net changes over the decade. Adding these changes in turn to our estimates of the 1950 census as corrected for under-enumeration provided our estimates of the "true" 1960 census populations. The differences represent the enumeration errors in the 1960 white population (for conterminous U.S.).

ADJUSTING MORTALITY RATES FOR UNDER-ENUMERATION

Our estimates of census enumeration errors imply that the estimates of survivorship we have used in our projections are in error.[6] The errors in survivorship (and consequently in our estimates of census enumeration errors) are greatest where: (a) under-enumeration is greatest, and (b) where survivorship is low.

The greater the under-enumeration, the greater the effect on mortality rates. However, the effect on survivorship is likely to be of little significance when survivorship rates are high. For example, if the proportion surviving some interval is .9800, allowance for a ten per cent undercount would raise the rate of survivorship only to .9820.

As a result, the effect of adjusting mortality for undercounts will be greater at old ages than at the young ages, because the survivorship rates are lower at the older ages and the rates of under-enumeration are greater (especially for the females) with age. Similarly, the effect is greater in the earlier censuses, because of the lower rates of survivorship and the higher levels of under-enumeration.

The estimates of census enumeration errors at the older ages are especially affected, not only because survivorship is likely to be low and under-enumeration high, but also because of the cumulative effect of the errors. For example, in projecting those

[6] This statement holds only for the period 1900–1950; before 1900 our estimates of survivorship are derived from model life tables and for the period 1950–1960 we have used estimates of absolute numbers of deaths. The reader should bear in mind that the adjustments and techniques described in the remainder of this chapter pertain to the period 1900–1950 (except for the brief discussion referring to the alternative 1960 estimates) and to birth cohorts alive as of 1900 or later.

See Chapter 5 for a discussion of the effect of using the original estimates of survivorship on our birth estimates and estimates of census enumeration errors.

age 55 in 1930 to age 65 in 1940, we have under-stated the expected number of survivors (because of the overstatement of mortality between ages 55 and 65); however, the number of survivors at age 55 in 1930 was already too small because of the error in projecting forward those age 45 in 1920, etc.

Our adjustments to the life tables for the enumeration errors were made in the following manner. For the six life tables centered on census years from 1900 to 1950, we estimated $_5m_x$ values from the $_5q_x$'s through the use of tables prepared by Reed and Merrell:[7] these $_5m_x$ values were then adjusted by the relevant age-sex-census enumeration errors (the 1900 values were applied to the 1900–1902 life tables; the difference of one year in the central date is certainly not important for the present purpose), and reconverted to $_5q_x$ values.[8] The remaining columns of the adjusted life tables were then completed (a minor adjustment was introduced to the $_5L_x$ column at the older ages to account for the nonlinearity of deaths).

ESTIMATING THE ALTERNATIVE SET OF CENSUS
ENUMERATION ERRORS

Ten-year life table survival ratios were then computed for five-year age-groups. The values, for the same age-group, in two successive life tables were averaged, thereby giving the average survivorship over a ten-year period for each age-group. For example,

$$\frac{\left(\dfrac{_5L_{50}}{_5L_{40}}\right)_{1930} + \left(\dfrac{_5L_{50}}{_5L_{40}}\right)_{1940}}{2}$$

equals the average survivorship rate between 1930 and 1940 of those 40–44 in 1930 (and therefore 50–54 in 1940). Generational survivorship rates were calculated by multiplying the appropriate average decade survivorship rates.

The same procedure was followed with the unadjusted life tables, i.e., the averaging of ten-year survivorship rates and the computation of generation rates. The ratio of the adjusted to the

[7] Lowell J. Reed, and Margaret Merrell, "A Short Method for Constructing an Abridged Life Table," *The American Journal of Hygiene*, Vol. XXX, No. 2 (September 1939), pp. 33–62.

[8] No adjustment was made to the $_5q_0$'s as the life tables were adjusted, in their construction, for under-enumeration at 0–4.

unadjusted rates was taken, giving the per cent by which survivorship had been understated in the unadjusted life tables due to under-enumeration of the population. These ratios were then multiplied by our original estimates of under-enumeration to give our alternative estimates.

To calculate the alternative estimates for 1960, we simply adjusted the 1950 total white population by our alternative estimates for 1950 and then carried through the same operations described above in the section pertaining to the expected 1960 population.

The following points should be noted about the technique described above:

a. We have assumed (as was implicitly true of our original estimates of enumeration errors) that registration of deaths was complete.

b. Unlike our original estimation procedure, we did not introduce any adjustments or corrections for the changing size of the Death Registration Area or for unusual mortality conditions occurring during a decade and not reflected in life tables centered on a census year (e.g., war losses). Since most of these adjustments had had only minor effects, and since the unadjusted and adjusted life tables were treated the same way for the alternative estimates, it is extremely unlikely that the omission of these adjustments has had any effect on our estimates.

c. In adjusting the life tables we made the same assumption that we had made in adjusting the total white population, namely, undercounts for age-groups born earlier than our earliest birth estimate were approximated by the estimated undercount from the earliest census in which an estimate for the given age-group was available. As a result, the numerator used in the computation of some survivorship ratios has been adjusted by a factor derived from a later census.

d. The alternative estimates for two age-groups (55–58 in 1910 and 65–68 in 1920) were prepared as if they covered five ages rather than four.

Terminating the Alternative Estimates

A major problem presents itself in this alternative estimation process, one which is especially troublesome at the older ages where we have originally estimated overcounts. We have, for example, estimated an overcount at age 70–74 in 1950 and adjusted the life table accordingly (i.e., by reducing survivorship). If those 70–74 in 1950 were actually undercounted, then we have made the existing error in survivorship even greater. That is, on the basis of the original mortality estimates, we have estimated an overcount for this group but we have no way of knowing how much of this overcount is a consequence of incorrect mortality. For the age-groups where the level of error but presumably not the direction of error is in question this problem is not of major significance (see immediately below). We have therefore terminated our alternative estimates at the age-group for which we originally estimated overcounts for the males (i.e., 70–74).

CONVERGENCE OF CONTINUED ESTIMATES

The process of estimating census enumeration errors, adjusting the life tables by these factors, and recomputing enumeration errors could have been continued. However, this process would quickly lead to a convergence (of the estimated enumeration errors) at the younger ages where, although the undercounts may be fairly substantial, the rate of survivorship is very high and not likely to be greatly influenced by the undercounts. At the older ages, the convergence would be somewhat slower, owing not only to the high rates of under-enumeration, but also to the low rates of survivorship. At those ages at which some uncertainty exists concerning the direction of error (i.e., 75–79 and over), adjustments in the wrong direction would lead to increasingly erroneous estimates.

APPENDICES

Appendix A. Special Adjustments

A number of special adjustments were necessary in utilizing and analyzing the reported single-year age distributions. Some of these adjustments are discussed in the text. The occasional repetition in this appendix of material already presented is in the interest of continuity of discussion.

1. DIFFERENCES IN CENSUS DATE AND QUESTION ON AGE

Differences in the time of year at which the various censuses were taken and, in one instance, a different question about age means that we cannot find an enumeration of precisely the same cohort in every census after its birth, and that the intercensal interval is not always precisely ten years.

The 1880, 1890, and 1900 censuses were taken as of June 1, the 1910 census as of April 15, the 1920 census as of January 1, and all other censuses from 1930 through 1960 as of April 1. The age question on every census except 1890 pertained to "age last birthday." In 1900 this question was supplemented by one asking for date of birth. In 1960, date of birth was asked *instead* of age, and age was determined by subtraction. The age so calculated was age last birthday. Persons whose age last birthday is x years have an exact age between x and $x + 1$, and a mean age of about $x + .5$ years.

In 1890, the age question pertained to "age at nearest birthday." Persons whose age at nearest birthday is x years have an exact age between $x - .5$ and $x + .5$, and a mean age of about x years. Persons born from December 1, 1884 to December 1, 1885 were reported as age 5 in 1890, if instructions were followed. The 1900 census was taken exactly 10 years later (as of June 1), but the persons reported as age 15 were not the same cohort reported as age 5 in 1890. Rather, the 15 year olds in the 1900 census were born between June 1, 1884 and June 1, 1885, and were six months younger than those reported at age 5 in 1890.

a. Effect on Age Ratios and Estimates of Age Heaping

The differences in the question pertaining to age and in the census dates necessitated approximations to arrive at roughly the same birth cohorts. In determining the age heaping adjustment factors, and the relative size of the birth cohorts, an attempt was made to make all of the measurements as of April 1, the most common of the census dates (in adjusting for age heaping the 1910 census was treated as if it had been taken on April 1, the difference of 14 days being considered insignificant). For example, of the cohort born April 1, 1874–March 31, 1875, $\frac{5}{6}$ were age 5 in 1880 and $\frac{1}{6}$ were age 6; in 1890 $\frac{1}{3}$ were age 15 while $\frac{2}{3}$ were age 16; in 1900 $\frac{5}{6}$ were age 25 and $\frac{1}{6}$ age 26; all were age 35 in 1910; in 1920 $\frac{1}{4}$ were age 44 and $\frac{3}{4}$ age 45; in 1930 all were age 55; in 1940, age 65; and in 1950, age 75. In measuring the deviation of an age ratio from its various trend lines it was not possible to take account of these differences.

It was however possible to allow for the differences in correcting the age ratios for the effect of cohort size. This was done by reallocating the cohorts by the proper weights—those given above.

b. *Effect on Estimates of Annual Births*

The same problem existed in preparing the estimates of annual births, i.e., it was necessary to convert estimates from the different censuses to January 1–December 31 figures. No adjustment was required for the estimates derived from the 1920 census; for the other censuses it was necessary to interpolate between estimates for two successive years, the weights used in each instance depending on the day the particular census was taken. In preparing the birth estimates, the actual date of the 1910 census was used, i.e., April 15. In estimating calendar-year births from this census, $\frac{17}{24}$ of one year's births was added to $\frac{7}{24}$ of the previous year's estimate.

This interpolation assumes a linear trend, during the year, of births and, where large variations are occurring, may decrease the reliability of the final estimates. At best, this process has the effect of reducing the annual variations.

c. *Effect on Estimates of Under-Enumeration*

The method of estimating "census-year" birth cohorts has been fully covered in the text.[1] The difference in census dates and in the age question forces the use of interpolation in estimating single-year expected populations. In addition, it was

[1] Pp. 148 to 149.

necessary to use, in the forward projections, the same estimates of mortality (actually relating to calendar-year periods) for all (roughly) comparable "census-year" estimates. For the more recent censuses any errors introduced by interpolation are reduced by the use of an adjustment factor derived from registered births. For all censuses we have shown estimates of under-enumeration by five-year age-groups rather than by single years. Errors in estimates for single years are probably compensating, rather than cumulative, over a five-year range (i.e., those errors arising from the interpolation process and the use of the calendar-year estimates of mortality). Use of five-year age-groups also seemed to justify the treatment, at this point, of the 1910 census as of April 1 rather than April 15.

2. Differences and Corrections of Reported Census Age Distributions for Native Whites

All of the material presented in this monograph deals with the area that was eventually to become "continental United States" (or what the Bureau of the Census defined as "conterminous United States" in the 1960 census), i.e., the District of Columbia and all states other than Alaska and Hawaii. However, persons born in Alaska and Hawaii (and other U.S. territories and possessions) have been listed as native in the censuses conducted since these areas came under U.S. jurisdiction. At the same time, persons born in the United States have not been included in the U.S. age distributions if they were residing outside of the United States at the time of the census. Thus native white age distributions for the U.S. in 1930, for example, include white persons born in Alaska and Hawaii (and other U.S. territories) if residing inside the U.S. and exclude persons born in the U.S. if, at the time of the census, they were residing elsewhere, including Alaska and Hawaii. No attempt was made in any of the censuses to reallocate these groups. The resulting errors in the various estimates represent the differences, by age and sex, between the two groups; it is highly unlikely that these errors are of any noticeable magnitude.

In addition to the issue discussed above, all censuses from 1900 on reported population abroad (i.e., outside of continental U.S. and U.S. territories and possessions). Except for 1920 and 1950 the number of such persons constituted a negligible proportion of the population residing in the United States, and only in 1950 was it possible to estimate, with some degree of accuracy, the size of the various age-sex-nativity groups abroad. For all of these censuses then the population abroad has been ignored. The treatment of the 1920 and 1950 censuses is given below.

a. *Age Unknown*

The censuses from 1890 through 1930 all contained the category "age unknown." Reapportioning these persons in the same way as those persons with a reported age would have had no effect on the age heaping ratios. At the same time, there did not seem to be any justification for reapportioning the unknowns in any other manner. As a result, persons reported as "age unknown" were not allocated to specific years.

This decision was carried through in preparing the birth estimates. The result here however, is to reduce somewhat the estimates. Because of the involved method of obtaining the final birth series, it was not possible to derive an estimate of the resulting error but it is undoubtedly small for any year. The estimates of under-enumeration are hardly affected since inclusion of the "age unknowns" for the birth estimates would also have increased the enumerated populations at the various ages. In other words, the expected populations would have been larger but so would the enumerated. In computing the total undercounts, by sex, for each census, the "age unknowns" have been included in the enumerated total, mainly for the purpose of having our tables agree with official figures.

b. *The 1890 Census*

In 1890 117,368 white persons were enumerated on Indian Territory and Indian Reservations.[2] These persons were not included in the totals for the United States nor was an age-sex-nativity cross-classification provided for them. Here again, no attempt was made to apportion these persons or to include them at any point in the computations. They were added, however, to the total enumerated white population (a sex-break was made by apportioning them to the two sexes in the same ratio as all non-Indians enumerated on Indian Territory, for whom a classifica-

[2] U.S. Census Office, 1890, *Report on Population of the United States*, Part I, Appendix, Table 1, p. 965.

tion by sex was provided) in obtaining our estimates of the total undercounts, by sex, for the 1890 census.

Two points should be kept in mind in reference to the effect of the omission of these persons on our estimates. The survivors of these persons were enumerated in subsequent censuses (if they were still residing in the United States). By being included in later enumerations, the native whites among these persons were used in estimating births. Secondly, the birth estimates derived from the 1890 males were not included in computing the final birth series. The effect then of omitting these persons is minimal on our birth estimates. At the same time, their omission had probably tended to increase slightly the age-sex estimates of under-enumeration in 1890.

c. The 1920 Census

In 1920 there was a total of 117,238 persons abroad,[3] with no age-sex-nativity classification provided. While the "reasonable assumption" might be that almost all of these persons were native white males in their 20's and 30's, this assumption was not made at this point and no adjustment was introduced to account for these persons in correcting for age heaping. Again, the omission of these persons has had little effect on our birth estimates since the native white survivors were included in subsequent census distributions, and since the 1920 males were not used in preparing our final birth series.

A different procedure from that used with the 1890 census was followed here in estimating undercounts. At this point we assumed that all of these persons were native white males, with an age distribution equal to that of the Armed Forces overseas in 1918. The estimated numbers abroad in each five-year age-group were *subtracted* from the estimated expected populations of native white males. The "net" expected populations were then used to estimate the undercounts of native white males.

d. The 1930 Census

In the 1930 census, Mexicans were not included as white, as they previously and subsequently were, but were classified as nonwhite under "other races." There was a total of 409,672

---

[3] U.S., Bureau of the Census, Population, Number and Distribution of Inhabitants, Vol. I, *1920 Census of Population*, Table 1, p. 13.

native male Mexicans and 395,482 native female Mexicans, shown only by a five-year age distribution. (These figures do not include those reported at "age unknown.")[4] Single-year estimates were arrived at by redistributing these numbers in the same proportion within each five-year age-group as the native whites of foreign or mixed parentage. These figures were then added to the figures given for native whites, the sum representing a total native population comparable to other censuses.

e. The 1940 Census

Single-year age distributions for the native white male and native white female populations are given in the 1940 census only for 35 years of age and over; under 35 years the classification is by five-year age-groups. There is, however, a single-year age distribution, by sex, for the total white population.[5] The numbers of foreign white up to age 29 were relatively small; only in the 30–34 years of age-group did they amount to significant proportions (7.5 per cent for the males and 7.9 per cent for the females). It therefore seemed justifiable to redistribute the 0–35 native whites to single years by the per cent distribution of total whites within each five-year age-group.

f. The 1950 Census

In the 1950 census, a total of 337,290 native white males were reported abroad.[6] Although this represents only 0.5 per cent of the total native white male population, there is a fairly high degree of concentration in the 20–34 years of age group. It therefore seemed advisable to make some adjustment to the figures shown for the native white males, which are only for "continental United States." No adjustment was made, at this point, for the native white females since the number abroad represented only 0.1 per cent of the total, with a somewhat smoother distribution over the entire age range.

The native white males abroad in the age ranges 0–14, and 40 and over, were allocated in the same proportions as the con-

---

[4] U.S., Bureau of the Census, *1930 Census of Population, op. cit.*, Table 15, p. 586.

[5] U.S., Bureau of the Census, *1940 Census of Population, op. cit.*, Table 2, p. 9.

[6] U.S., Bureau of the Census, *1950 Census of Population, op. cit.*, Table 35, pp. 1–87.

tinental native white males, and those 15–39 were assigned the age distribution of white males in the Armed Forces stationed in continental United States. This latter distribution was determined by subtracting the civilian labor force from the total labor force.

The 1950 native white age distributions were based on a 20 per cent sample of the total population. Because of the way the sample was selected, certain biases are present in these distributions. Put simply, the sample contained too many children and too many old people, and too few young adults, especially male adults. For example, the sample age distribution shows more native whites under 1 year of age than the complete count shows under 1 year of age for total whites, native and foreign-born.

It therefore seemed advisable to adjust the sample distributions. The ratio of total white males from the complete count, to total white males from the 20 per cent sample was computed and used to adjust the native white males from the 20 per cent sample. This adjustment provided an estimated "native white male age distribution from the complete count." In making this adjustment the age-groups used varied from single-years to five-year groups, depending on the age classifications provided in the official census tabulations.

The native white males abroad were added to this estimated complete count. This total population was then adjusted for age heaping, the correction factors being those originally calculated using the sample age distribution. From this point on, the techniques involved in projecting backward and forward were those described in the text. A similar adjustment was made to the native white female age distribution, including the estimation and inclusion of the native white females abroad. In one respect the adjustments to the females differ from the adjustments to the males—in the case of the males the population abroad was included in estimating age heaping and in estimating births, while the females abroad were included only in estimating the births and not in determining the age heaping correction factors.

In computing the estimated undercounts in this census, the numbers abroad were *subtracted* from the estimated expected populations. The number subtracted at each age was the same as had been added to the enumerated continental populations.

Appendix B. Construction of Life Tables

The decade life tables we have used in preparing the various estimates of births and under-enumeration are of two types. Model life tables have been used for the nineteenth century because of the unavailability of mortality records for this country during that century. The establishment of the Death Registration Area in 1900 has enabled us to utilize official tables for the twentieth century. It has been necessary in some instances, however, to construct decade life tables from three-year life tables centered on years ending in zero and to adjust some of the life tables to represent continental United States.[1]

1. CONSTRUCTION OF MODEL LIFE TABLES FOR THE 19TH CENTURY

The absence of mortality records covering a major proportion of the American population before 1900 caused us to estimate mortality indirectly, from model life tables. We could have employed the tables published by the United Nations,[2] but preferred to use our own for these reasons:

The U.N. model life tables are based on 158 national life tables from all parts of the world, representing exclusively twentieth century experience. The age-patterns of mortality in the high mortality model tables are strongly influenced by Indian life tables, which by the nature of their construction do not have age-patterns of reliable accuracy. (The Indian tables are based on survivorship from one census to the next of populations with conspicuously deficient age reporting, hence the age-pattern of mortality rates depends heavily on rather arbitrary adjustments made in the reported age distributions.) Thus the U.N. collection is not on the face of it likely to be representative of age-patterns of mortality in the United States in the nineteenth century.

The tables we employed were based on 138 life tables, all from Western Europe plus overseas areas settled by West Europeans (Australia, New Zealand, the United States, and Canada). Thirty-six of them represent nineteenth century experience. The method of construction was to order the q_x values ($_1q_0$, $_4q_1$, and

---

[1] See pp. 7 and 8.
[2] United Nations, *Age and Sex Patterns of Mortality*. Document ST/SOA/Series A. Population Studies No. 22.

$_5q_x$, $x = 5$ to 75) from highest to lowest at each age, and to form one table from the tenth highest rate at each age, another from the twentieth rate at each age, etc.

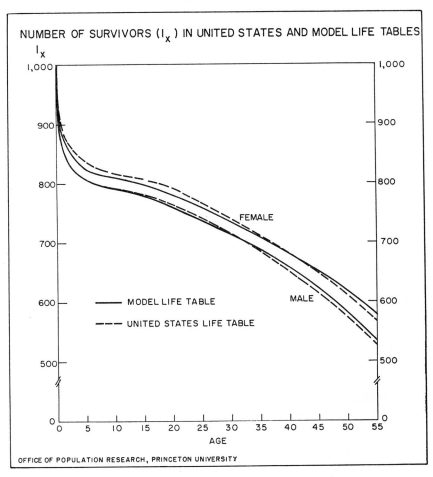

NUMBER OF SURVIVORS (l_x) IN UNITED STATES AND MODEL LIFE TABLES

OFFICE OF POPULATION RESEARCH, PRINCETON UNIVERSITY

FIGURE 58. l_x Values, by Sex, in 1901 United States
Life Tables and Model Life Tables with Same $\mathring{e}_0$'s.

The suitability of these tables for estimating survivorship in the United States late in the nineteenth century is indicated indirectly by a comparison of l_x values in the 1900 U.S. life table and the model life table with the same expectation of life at birth (Figure 58).

Tables 10 and 11 show the life tables employed to estimate

survivorship in each decade from 1850 to 1900. The level of mortality was determined by estimates of the expectation of life at birth for each sex (see page 8). Actually, the only relevant values are survivorship to age 5 in the 1850's, age 15 in the 1860's, and to age 45 in the 1890's.

TABLE 10
Model Life Table l_x Values Used for Native White Male Projections 1850–1900

Age	1855	1865	1875	1885	1895
0	1000	1000	1000	1000	1000
5	731	749	767	784	802
10	703	723	743	764	784
15	689	710	731	752	773
20	670	691	712	734	755
25	643	664	686	709	731
30	615	638	660	683	706
35	588	611	634	657	680
40	557	581	604	628	651
45	523	547	570	594	617
50	483	507	530	554	577

TABLE 11
Model Life Table l_x Values Used for Native White Female Projections 1850–1900

Age	1855	1865	1875	1885	1895
0	1000	1000	1000	1000	1000
5	755	772	790	807	823
10	728	747	767	786	805
15	712	732	753	772	791
20	691	711	733	753	773
25	667	688	710	730	750
30	641	662	685	706	726
35	613	635	658	679	700
40	583	606	628	651	673
45	551	574	598	620	643
50	517	541	564	587	610

2. CONSTRUCTION AND ADJUSTMENT OF DECADE LIFE TABLES FOR THE 20TH CENTURY

The first decade life table for continental United States covers the period 1930–1939.[3] No such table was prepared for the

[3] U.S., Bureau of the Census, *United States Life Tables, 1930–1939 (Preliminary) for White and Nonwhite by Sex,* prepared by Elbertie Foudray and Thomas N. E. Greville, Tables 1 and 2.

1940's; it was however possible to utilize the 1939–1941 life table[4] and the 1949–1951 life table[5] to approximate one covering the decade. This was accomplished by averaging the $_1p_x$ values for each year of age and then computing values of l_x and $_1L_x$ on the basis of these $_1p_x$'s.

For the decade of the 1920's there is available a life table for 1920–1929 but covering only the Death Registration states of 1920.[6] To adjust this life table so as to be representative of continental United States, the ratio of the $_1p_x$'s for the total United States life table for 1929–1931[7] to the $_1p_x$'s for the 1929–1931 life table for the registration states of 1920[8] was taken; this ratio was then used to adjust the $_1p_x$'s of the 1920–1929 life table. This of course is on the assumption that the differences between the two 1929–1931 life tables, reflecting differences in the mortality experience of the continental United States as contrasted to that which occurred in the Death Registration states of 1920, were the same over the entire decade. Most of the adjustment factors were of negligible proportions and nowhere reached 1 per cent.

For the 1910's it was necessary to average the 1909–1911 life table[9] and the 1919–1921 life table[10] after each had been adjusted to represent the continental United States. The former covered only the Original Registration states. In this instance the adjustment factor was estimated by the ratio of the $_1p_x$'s in the 1929–1931 continental United States life tables to the $_1p_x$'s in the 1929–1931 life table for the Original Registration states,[11] the ratio then being applied to the 1909–1911 life table. The 1919–1921 life table covered the Death Registration states of 1920 and was adjusted by the same factors used to adjust the 1920–1929 life table.

The 1901–1910 life table[12] also covered the Original Death

[4] U.S., Bureau of the Census, "United States Life Tables 1939–1941," *Vital Statistics—Special Reports*, Vol. 19, No. 4 (1944), Tables 1 and 2.

[5] U.S., National Office of Vital Statistics, "United States Life Tables 1949–1951," *Vital Statistics—Special Reports*, Vol. 41, No. 1 (1954), Tables 5 and 6.

[6] U.S., Bureau of the Census, *United States Life Tables: 1929 to 1931, 1920 to 1929, 1919 to 1921, 1909 to 1911, 1901 to 1910, 1900 to 1902*, prepared by Joseph A. Hill, Tables III-A and III-B.

[7] *Ibid.*, Tables I-A and I-B.

[8] *Ibid.*, Tables II-A and II-B.

[9] *Ibid.*, Tables VI-A and VI-B.

[10] *Ibid.*, Tables IV-A and IV-B.

[11] *Ibid.*, Tables V-A and V-B.

[12] *Ibid.*, Tables VII-A and VII-B.

Registration states and was corrected by the factors used to correct the 1909–1911 life table.

The various corrections were small and were made largely for the purpose of consistency in providing a series of decade life tables from 1901–1910 to 1940–1950 which covered the same area. It should be noted however, that all of the life tables used were for whites and not for native whites. No correction was derived for this condition for two reasons; (1) the only separate life tables by nativity are for 1901 and 1910, and (2) a comparison of age-specific death rates for native whites (by sex) and total whites (by sex) reveals very minor differences, making justifiable the use of life tables for total whites.[13]

[13] U.S., Bureau of the Census, *Vital Statistics Rates in the United States, 1900–1940*, prepared by Forrest E. Linder and Robert D. Grove, Table 9.

Appendix C. Detailed Tables

TABLE 12
Estimated Native White Males, by Single Years of Age, 1880–1950[a]
(000's Omitted—Rounded to Three Figures)[b]

	Census							
Age	1880	1890	1900	1910	1920	1930	1940	1950
0	698	437	931	1,110	1,140	1,090	1,060	1,570
1	640	816	862	1,040	1,160	1,080	1,040	1,550
2	625	766	835	998	1,140	1,130	1,010	1,600
3	612	734	833	964	1,100	1,110	962	1,620
4	608	714	828	937	1,090	1,120	971	1,200
5	586	703	816	897	1,080	1,160	996	1,240
6	572	691	813	878	1,060	1,150	928	1,280
7	562	669	810	846	1,050	1,120	961	1,310
8	544	646	783	813	1,020	1,190	1,000	1,150
9	524	630	742	840	1,000	1,150	1,040	1,070
10	513	606	739	825	1,010	1,110	1,050	1,030
11	491	592	730	803	983	1,090	1,060	1,020
12	481	583	703	795	953	1,110	1,110	995
13	463	583	683	804	927	1,080	1,090	952
14	433	579	679	801	901	1,060	1,100	962
15	407	573	670	790	864	1,060	1,140	986
16	393	556	656	789	843	1,040	1,130	919
17	408	544	627	785	810	1,030	1,110	944
18	428	532	614	754	784	1,000	1,170	972
19	433	513	590	713	802	980	1,130	1,010
20	415	497	571	714	775	985	1,090	993
21	402	483	552	699	757	962	1,070	1,010
22	392	463	547	670	747	931	1,090	1,070
23	371	451	540	650	752	903	1,050	1,060
24	356	424	543	646	745	879	1,040	1,070
25	344	396	526	634	735	841	1,030	1,100
26	323	375	513	617	733	822	1,020	1,090
27	300	374	503	588	722	790	1,000	1,060
28	280	390	486	576	688	752	974	1,130
29	277	402	468	554	659	774	951	1,090
30		395	457	537	658	757	955	1,050
31		380	436	520	640	733	932	1,030
32		370	424	520	615	722	902	1,050
33		355	407	510	600	726	874	1,020
34		337	379	509	593	721	849	1,000

(CONTINUED)

TABLE 12 (CONTINUED)

Age	Census							
	1880	1890	1900	1910	1920	1930	1940	1950
35		325	355	489	582	709	811	999
36		309	341	476	562	704	792	982
37		289	353	464	539	698	760	970
38		268	368	447	525	668	722	941
39		257	371	429	504	629	741	918
40			354	417	491	627	723	920
41			343	396	478	612	698	897
42			333	385	475	584	685	865
43			313	366	467	565	687	836
44			300	340	460	558	680	810
45			288	318	442	546	666	772
46			268	307	429	529	659	750
47			248	318	417	501	650	717
48			230	330	399	489	618	678
49			226	328	382	467	579	692
50				312	370	450	573	671
51				301	352	432	556	644
52				290	339	429	527	627
53				271	318	417	506	624
54				259	294	412	496	612
55				246	274	392	480	594
56				227	268	377	461	582
57				208	275	363	433	568
58				192	280	345	417	534
59					272	326	394	494
60					257	312	375	483
61					244	292	355	461
62					230	278	347	430
63					213	258	331	406
64					199	234	321	391
65					184	213	300	372
66					166	200	282	350
67					149	200	266	321
68					136	200	246	303
69						191	226	278
70						174	210	258
71						160	190	237
72						146	174	224
73						129	156	206
74						116	135	193

(CONTINUED)

TABLE 12 (CONCLUDED)

| | | | | | Census | | |
Age	1880	1890	1900	1910	1920	1930	1940	1950
75						102	117	172
76						87.6	104	154
77						73.9	98.5	138
78						62.3	92.4	120
79							82.5	104
80							69.7	90.1
81							59.1	75.6
82							49.5	64.2
83							39.8	52.5
84							32.2	41.5
85							25.6	32.5
86							19.5	26.0
87							14.5	21.8
88							10.7	18.0
89								14.0
90								10.3
91								7.5
92								5.3
93								3.6
94								2.5
95								1.6
96								1.0
97								.6
98								.4

[a] These estimates are based on the use of unadjusted life tables for the period 1900–1950; see pp. 154–155.

[b] Except at highest ages in 1950 where only one or two significant figures are carried.

TABLE 13
Estimated Native White Females, by Single Years of Age, 1880–1950[a]
(000's Omitted—Rounded to Three Figures)[b]

	Census							
Age	1880	1890	1900	1910	1920	1930	1940	1950
0	669	417	892	1,060	1,090	1,040	1,010	1,500
1	618	786	831	1,010	1,120	1,040	993	1,480
2	605	740	806	966	1,100	1,080	965	1,530
3	593	710	805	936	1,060	1,070	923	1,540
4	589	691	801	910	1,050	1,080	933	1,140
5	569	681	789	869	1,040	1,110	952	1,180
6	555	669	786	850	1,030	1,100	887	1,220
7	546	648	784	820	1,010	1,080	919	1,250
8	528	626	757	789	985	1,140	958	1,100
9	510	610	718	814	972	1,110	1,000	1,020
10	499	588	715	800	975	1,070	1,000	985
11	478	574	706	778	954	1,060	1,020	983
12	467	565	680	770	927	1,080	1,060	957
13	450	565	661	778	903	1,050	1,050	917
14	420	561	656	776	878	1,030	1,060	927
15	395	555	648	766	844	1,030	1,100	946
16	381	539	634	764	822	1,010	1,090	881
17	396	528	607	761	792	1,000	1,070	913
18	415	516	595	731	773	972	1,130	951
19	421	497	574	691	789	954	1,090	992
20	403	482	556	692	769	956	1,050	995
21	392	469	541	679	751	936	1,040	1,010
22	382	450	540	650	742	908	1,060	1,050
23	362	438	532	631	747	882	1,030	1,040
24	348	413	533	627	740	858	1,010	1,050
25	336	386	516	616	729	820	1,010	1,080
26	316	366	503	599	726	800	990	1,070
27	294	365	493	571	714	770	977	1,050
28	274	381	476	560	680	739	948	1,110
29	271	393	459	538	651	759	929	1,080
30		387	448	522	649	743	931	1,040
31		372	427	506	631	720	911	1,030
32		362	416	506	605	709	882	1,040
33		348	399	497	591	714	856	1,010
34		331	371	497	584	709	833	992
35		319	348	479	572	697	795	988
36		303	335	466	553	692	774	971
37		283	347	456	531	686	744	958
38		263	362	439	517	656	713	928
39		252	366	422	497	618	732	909

(CONTINUED)

TABLE 13 (CONTINUED)

Age					Census			
	1880	1890	1900	1910	1920	1930	1940	1950
40			349	412	483	617	715	909
41			338	392	471	603	692	889
42			329	382	469	576	680	859
43			310	363	462	557	684	833
44			297	338	457	552	677	808
45			286	317	440	540	664	769
46			268	307	428	524	658	748
47			248	318	417	498	651	717
48			230	331	399	486	620	685
49			227	330	384	465	582	701
50				314	373	449	578	683
51				304	355	433	563	658
52				293	343	431	535	645
53				275	322	420	515	645
54				263	298	416	507	636
55				250	279	398	493	620
56				232	274	384	475	611
57				213	282	372	448	600
58				198	288	355	434	568
59					281	337	412	530
60					266	324	394	522
61					254	304	375	503
62					240	291	369	473
63					223	271	355	450
64					210	247	347	438
65					195	226	326	421
66					177	213	309	399
67					160	215	294	371
68					147	216	274	353
69						207	254	328
70						190	238	307
71						176	217	285
72						162	201	273
73						144	181	254
74						130	158	240
75						116	139	217
76						101	125	197
77						85.7	119	179
78						73.1	113	158
79							102	139

(CONTINUED)

TABLE 13 (CONCLUDED)

	Census							
Age	1880	1890	1900	1910	1920	1930	1940	1950
80							87.0	122
81							74.7	104
82							63.4	89.2
83							51.7	74.0
84							42.5	59.3
85							34.3	47.3
86							26.6	38.3
87							20.1	32.7
88							15.1	27.5
89								21.9
90								16.3
91								12.1
92								8.8
93								6.1
94								4.2
95								2.8
96								1.8
97								1.1
98								.7

[a] These estimates are based on the use of unadjusted life tables for the period 1900–1950; see pp. 154–155.

[b] Except at highest ages in 1950 where only one or two significant figures are carried.

TABLE 14
Estimated Per Cent Census Enumeration Errors for Native White Males,
by 5-Year Age-Groups, 1880–1950[a]
(− Indicates Overcount, i.e., Enumerated Population Larger Than
Estimated Population)

	Census							
Age	1880	1890	1900	1910	1920	1930	1940	1950
0–4	9.1	4.8	7.6	7.9	7.6	7.7	7.1	4.5
5–9	3.5	5.9	4.6	3.4	4.0	3.2	4.2	3.1
10–14	0.8	3.5	5.1	5.3	4.5	2.5	3.4	0.8
15–19	5.2	6.2	5.7	5.0	5.7	3.4	4.5	4.1
20–24	−0.5	2.4	2.4	4.1	6.0	6.5	6.4	5.9
25–29	3.5	7.4	6.1	6.0	7.1	6.0	5.9	5.2
30–34		11.2	7.4	7.8	9.8	6.9	6.6	4.5
35–39		8.2	6.0	4.2	2.1	3.6	2.7	2.2
40–44			9.7	6.7	8.6	5.9	4.0	3.5
45–49			6.5	6.4	1.7	4.6	4.8	2.1
50–54				3.1	1.8	2.0	3.5	2.1
55–59				6.8[b]	10.7	7.7	6.3	5.3
60–64					6.9	5.1	4.2	3.4
65–69					5.7[c]	6.0	0.4	−0.6
70–74						4.7	−1.0	−1.2
75–79						1.3[d]	1.5	−3.2
80–84							0.0	−7.9
85–89							−3.5[e]	−6.3
90–94								−5.9
95–99								−28.3[f]

[a] These estimates are based on the use of unadjusted life tables for the period 1900–1950; see pp. 154–155.
[b] 55–58 years.
[c] 65–68 years.
[d] 75–78 years.
[e] 85–88 years.
[f] 95–98 years.

TABLE 15
Estimated Per Cent Census Enumeration Errors for Native White Females,
by 5-Year Age Groups, 1880–1950[a]
(— Indicates Overcount, i.e., Enumerated Population Larger Than
Estimated Population)

	Census							
Age	1880	1890	1900	1910	1920	1930	1940	1950
0–4	9.1	5.0	6.5	7.4	6.6	6.6	6.6	3.9
5–9	3.2	5.2	3.6	2.5	2.8	2.1	3.1	2.3
10–14	1.5	3.7	4.0	4.5	3.7	1.7	2.5	0.8
15–19	0.1	1.6	2.1	1.8	3.0	0.9	2.1	1.9
20–24	−2.2	−0.6	−0.9	−0.9	1.4	1.2	1.4	1.7
25–29	6.7	6.9	5.8	3.3	3.4	1.2	1.4	0.3
30–34		16.1	10.1	7.4	7.0	3.7	3.4	0.0
35–39		15.3	10.1	7.1	3.8	2.0	0.4	−1.4
40–44			17.0	11.6	9.3	5.9	3.4	2.0
45–49			16.4	13.7	11.6	6.9	5.7	1.5
50–54				16.8	12.1	7.3	5.9	2.7
55–59				21.5[b]	21.0	15.6	10.2	7.6
60–64					20.9	13.8	9.0	7.2
65–69					19.7[c]	14.7	6.3	1.9
70–74						16.5	7.6	4.4
75–79						11.7[d]	8.4	3.9
80–84							5.4	−1.3
85–89							−0.3[e]	−4.7
90–94								−7.9
95–99								−24.0[f]

[a] These estimates are based on the use of unadjusted life tables for the period
1900–1950; see pp. 154–155.

[b] 55–58 years.

[c] 65–68 years.

[d] 75–78 years.

[e] 85–88 years.

[f] 95–98 years.

TABLE 16
Estimated Total White Males, by 5-Year Age Groups, 1880–1950[a]
(000's Omitted—Rounded to Three Figures)

Age	1880	1890	1900	1910	1920	1930	1940	1950
0–4	3,220	3,510	4,320	5,100	5,660	5,560	5,040	7,570
5–9	2,850	3,470	4,040	4,430	5,300	5,840	4,940	6,100
10–14	2,500	3,150	3,700	4,220	4,950	5,550	5,440	4,980
15–19	2,260	2,990	3,440	4,200	4,380	5,310	5,760	4,880
20–24	2,210	2,810	3,220	4,240	4,260	5,060	5,440	5,300
25–29	1,900	2,590	3,120	4,020	4,380	4,580	5,180	5,630
30–34	1,720[b]	2,450	2,810	3,550	4,150	4,400	4,880	5,310
35–39	1,460[b]	1,980	2,500	3,150	3,740	4,380	4,370	5,060
40–44	1,220[c]	1,640[c]	2,250	2,710	3,240	4,000	4,150	4,730
45–49	1,020[c]	1,350[c]	1,760	2,300	2,830	3,480	4,030	4,170
50–54	883[d]	1,120[d]	1,440[d]	1,980	2,330	2,890	3,570	3,840
55–59	675[e]	878[e]	1,150[e]	1,510[e]	1,930	2,410	2,970	3,530
60–64	552[e]	734[e]	882[e]	1,150[e]	1,560	1,890	2,330	2,930
65–69	362[f]	508[f]	645[f]	840[f]	1,060[f]	1,410	1,740	2,210
70–74	235[f]	349[f]	431[f]	543[f]	687[f]	981	1,170	1,500
75–79	128[g]	186[g]	244[g]	312[g]	397[g]	524[g]	692	899
80–84	59.6[g]	88.6[g]	110[g]	141[g]	172[g]	235[g]	339	440
85+	23.8[h]	37.3[h]	42.0[h]	60.5[h]	74.7[h]	97.6[h]	131[h]	203[h]
Total	23,300	29,800	36,100	44,500	51,100	58,600	62,200	69,300

[a] These estimates are based on the error rates presented in Table 14.
[b] Adjusted by error estimated for this age group in the 1890 census.
[c] Adjusted by error estimated for this age group in the 1900 census.
[d] Adjusted by error estimated for this age group in the 1910 census.
[e] Adjusted by error estimated for this age group in the 1920 census.
[f] Adjusted by error estimated for this age group in the 1930 census.
[g] Adjusted by error estimated for this age group in the 1940 census.
[h] Adjusted by error estimated for 85–98 in the 1950 census.

TABLE 17
Estimated Total White Females, by 5-Year Age-Groups, 1880–1950[a]
(000's Omitted—Rounded to Three Figures)

Age	1880	1890	1900	1910	1920	1930	1940	1950
0–4	3,110	3,390	4,160	4,930	5,450	5,310	4,830	7,210
5–9	2,770	3,360	3,910	4,290	5,130	5,620	4,730	5,810
10–14	2,430	3,060	3,580	4,090	4,810	5,370	5,220	4,790
15–19	2,200	2,900	3,350	4,040	4,300	5,160	5,560	4,730
20–24	2,140	2,690	3,160	3,880	4,230	4,920	5,300	5,260
25–29	1,820	2,390	2,980	3,580	4,180	4,440	5,080	5,590
30–34	1,660[b]	2,260	2,630	3,190	3,810	4,250	4,790	5,280
35–39	1,490[b]	1,860	2,310	2,900	3,430	4,130	4,280	5,030
40–44	1,260[c]	1,600[c]	2,100	2,500	3,030	3,700	4,070	4,710
45–49	1,050[c]	1,370[c]	1,690	2,160	2,690	3,270	3,900	4,150
50–54	901[d]	1,180[d]	1,450[d]	1,910	2,270	2,800	3,420	3,880
55–59	659[e]	893[e]	1,240[e]	1,450[e]	1,890	2,400	2,910	3,600
60–64	557[e]	770[e]	962[e]	1,200[e]	1,580	1,930	2,380	3,030
65–69	362[f]	512[f]	673[f]	869[f]	1,060[f]	1,470	1,870	2,410
70–74	256[f]	360[f]	478[f]	596[f]	749[f]	1,080	1,310	1,740
75–79	140[g]	193[g]	257[g]	340[g]	445[g]	572[g]	799	1,120
80–84	71.5[g]	99.8[g]	121[g]	162[g]	212[g]	279[g]	414	587
85+	31.9[h]	47.4[h]	52.3[h]	73.8[h]	98.5[h]	131[h]	177[h]	295[h]
Total	22,900	28,900	35,100	42,200	49,400	56,800	61,000	69,200

[a] These estimates are based on the error rates presented in Table 15.

[b] Adjusted by error estimated for this age group in the 1890 census.

[c] Adjusted by error estimated for this age group in the 1900 census.

[d] Adjusted by error estimated for this age group in the 1910 census.

[e] Adjusted by error estimated for this age group in the 1920 census.

[f] Adjusted by error estimated for this age group in the 1930 census.

[g] Adjusted by error estimated for this age group in the 1940 census.

[h] Adjusted by error estimated for 85–98 in the 1950 census.

TABLE 18
Estimated and Enumerated Total White Population; by Age and Sex,
(for Conterminous U.S.), April 1, 1960
(000's Omitted)[a]

	Male			Female		
Age	Census Count	Estimated Population	Error as % of Census	Census Count	Estimated Population	Error as % of Census
0–4[b]	8,823	9,020	2.2	8,485	8,600	1.4
5–9[b]	8.182	8,350	2.0	7,866	7,960	1.2
10–14	7,441	7,600	2.1	7,167	7,250	1.1
15–19	5,818	6,040	3.8	5,761	5,880	2.0
20–24	4,614	4,780	3.6	4,811	4,930	2.5
25–29	4,702	4,880	3.8	4,819	4,860	0.9
30–34	5,201	5,470	5.1	5,357	5,410	1.0
35–39	5,430	5,700	5.0	5,680	5,700	0.3
40–44	5,103	5,270	3.3	5,295	5,270	−0.5
45–49	4,818	4,960	2.9	4,949	4,990	0.8
50–54	4,278	4,470	4.6	4,401	4,600	4.4
55–59	3,723	3,740	0.5	3,893	3,950	1.5
60–64	3,118	3,230	3.6	3,426	3,590	4.8
65–69	2,682	2,710	0.9	3,053	3,150	3.1
70–74	2,017	1,950	−3.3	2,371	2,400	1.4
75–79	1,254	1,220	−3.0	1,579	1,660	5.3
80–84	619	590	−4.7	861	921	7.0
85+	331	240	−27.5	526	468	−11.0
Total	78,154	80,200	2.6	80,300	81,600	1.6

[a] The estimated populations are rounded to three figures.
[b] Alternative figures that make allowance for overseas births 1950–1959 are as follows:

	Male			Female		
Age	Census Count	Estimated Population	Error as % of Census	Census Count	Estimated Population	Error as % of Census
0–4	8,823	9,110	3.3	8,485	8,690	2.5
5–9	8,182	8,410	2.8	7,866	8,020	1.9

See p. 52.

TABLE 19
l_x and $_5q_x$ Values for White Males in U.S. Life Tables Adjusted for Under-Enumeration, 1901–1950

Life Table

	1901		1910		1920	
Age	l_x	$_5q_x$	l_x	$_5q_x$	l_x	$_5q_x$
0	1,000	.191	1,000	.170	1,000	.112
5	809	.021	830	.169	888	.014
10	792	.013	816	.011	876	.011
15	782	.020	807	.017	866	.017
20	766	.032	793	.025	851	.021
25	742	.034	773	.027	833	.024
30	716	.039	752	.033	813	.027
35	689	.046	727	.043	791	.034
40	657	.050	696	.051	764	.037
45	625	.063	660	.063	736	.048
50	585	.081	619	.082	700	.064
55	538	.103	568	.107	655	.085
60	482	.145	507	.155	600	.125
65	412	.208	429	.216	525	.183
70	327	.288	336	.303	429	.274
75	233	.422	234	.432	312	.391
80	135	.572	133	.577	190	.538
85	58	.735	56	.729	88	.711
90	15		15		25	

Life Table

	1930		1940		1950	
Age	l_x	$_5q_x$	l_x	$_5q_x$	l_x	$_5q_x$
0	1,000	.083	1,000	.058	1,000	.036
5	917	.009	942	.005	964	.003
10	908	.008	936	.005	961	.004
15	901	.012	931	.008	957	.006
20	890	.016	924	.011	952	.008
25	876	.018	914	.012	944	.008
30	860	.021	903	.014	936	.009
35	842	.027	890	.020	927	.014
40	819	.036	872	.029	914	.023
45	790	.049	846	.043	893	.037
50	751	.070	810	.064	860	.058
55	698	.095	758	.092	810	.080
60	632	.138	688	.134	745	.134
65	545	.198	595	.197	646	.187
70	437	.284	478	.288	525	.266
75	313	.411	340	.401	385	.380
80	184	.560	204	.546	239	.527
85	81	.714	93	.713	113	.676
90	23		27		37	

TABLE 20
l_x and $_5q_x$ Values for White Females in U.S. Life Tables Adjusted for
Under-Enumeration, 1901–1950

Life Table

	1901		1910		1920	
Age	l_x	$_5q_x$	l_x	$_5q_x$	l_x	$_5q_x$
0	1,000	.166	1,000	.147	1,000	.093
5	834	.020	853	.016	907	.012
10	818	.012	840	.010	896	.009
15	808	.021	832	.016	888	.016
20	791	.031	819	.023	874	.024
25	767	.033	800	.027	853	.028
30	741	.035	778	.029	830	.028
35	715	.038	756	.035	806	.031
40	687	.040	729	.038	781	.032
45	660	.048	702	.046	756	.039
50	628	.062	669	.058	726	.052
55	590	.081	630	.080	689	.066
60	542	.110	580	.114	643	.096
65	482	.170	513	.177	581	.153
70	400	.239	423	.249	492	.227
75	305	.368	317	.374	381	.349
80	192	.514	199	.530	248	.497
85	94	.698	93	.702	125	.682
90	28		28		40	

Life Table

	1930		1940		1950	
Age	l_x	$_5q_x$	l_x	$_5q_x$	l_x	$_5q_x$
0	1,000	.068	1,000	.047	1,000	.028
5	932	.008	953	.004	972	.002
10	925	.006	949	.004	970	.002
15	919	.010	945	.006	968	.003
20	909	.016	940	.008	965	.004
25	895	.017	932	.010	961	.005
30	880	.019	923	.011	956	.007
35	863	.023	913	.015	950	.009
40	843	.028	899	.020	941	.014
45	820	.036	880	.028	928	.021
50	790	.050	855	.042	908	.032
55	750	.067	820	.059	879	.046
60	700	.100	771	.090	838	.072
65	630	.151	702	.142	777	.118
70	535	.219	603	.218	686	.187
75	418	.351	471	.329	558	.291
80	271	.506	316	.479	395	.443
85	134	.683	165	.673	220	.617
90	43		54		84	

TABLE 21

Estimated Per Cent Census Enumeration Errors Based on Life Tables Adjusted
for Under-Enumeration, Native White Males, 1910–1950
and Total White Males, 1960

Age	1910	1920	1930	1940	1950	1960
10–14	5.4	4.6	2.5	3.4		
15–19	4.9	5.7	3.4	4.5	4.1	
20–24	4.2	6.3	6.7	6.5	6.0	
25–29	6.3	7.3	6.2	6.0	5.3	3.8
30–34	8.2	10.5	7.5	7.0	4.7	5.2
35–39	4.7	2.9	4.2	3.1	2.4	5.0
40–44	7.3	9.6	6.7	4.7	3.9	3.5
45–49	7.3	2.8	5.8	5.6	2.6	3.1
50–54	3.8	2.9	3.2	4.7	3.0	5.0
55–59	7.9	12.4	9.4	8.1	6.8	1.0
60–64		9.6	7.7	6.6	5.7	4.7
65–69		9.3	8.6	3.4	1.7	2.8
70–74			10.1	3.0	1.0	0.0

TABLE 22

Estimated Per Cent Census Enumeration Errors Based on Life Tables Adjusted
for Under-Enumeration, Native White Females, 1910–1950
and Total White Females, 1960

Age	1910	1920	1930	1940	1950	1960
10–14	4.6	3.8	1.7	2.5		
15–19	1.7	2.9	0.9	2.1	1.9	
20–24	−0.9	1.5	1.3	1.4	1.7	
25–29	3.4	3.4	1.2	1.4	0.3	0.9
30–34	7.7	7.3	3.9	3.5	0.0	1.0
35–39	7.7	4.3	2.2	0.4	−1.4	0.3
40–44	12.5	10.2	6.4	3.7	2.1	−0.5
45–49	15.1	13.2	7.9	6.1	1.6	0.8
50–54	18.9	13.8	8.9	6.9	3.2	4.5
55–59	24.8	25.1	18.8	11.5	8.5	1.6
60–64		27.8	18.8	12.5	9.0	5.3
65–69		29.6	23.6	12.1	4.2	4.1
70–74			31.1	17.1	9.4	3.5